Helion & Company Limited
Unit 8 Amherst Business Centre
Budbrooke Road
Warwick
CV34 5WE
England
Tel. 01926 499 619
Email: info@helion.co.uk
Website: www.helion.co.uk
Twitter: @helionbooks
Visit our blog http://blog.helion.co.uk/

Published by Helion & Company 2024
Designed and typeset by Farr out
    Publications, Wokingham, Berkshire
Cover designed by Paul Hewitt, Battlefield
    Design (www.battlefield-design.co.uk)

Text © Antonio Luis Sapienza Fracchia 2024
Illustrations © as individually credited
Colour artwork by Luca Canossa, Tom
    Cooper and Ivan Zajac 2024
Maps by the author 2024

ISBN 978-1-804514-66-5

British Library Cataloguing-in-Publication
    Data
A catalogue record for this book is available
    from the British Library

We always welcome receiving book
proposals from prospective authors.

CONTENTS

ABBREVIATIONS AND ACRONYMS

ACH	*Armada de Chile*/Chilean Navy		**GDT**	*Grupo de Tareas*/Task Force Group (Argentina)
ARA	*Armada de la República Argentina*/Argentine Navy		**IAI**	Israel Aircraft Industries
AMD-BA	*Avions Marcel Dassault-Breguet Aviation* (France)		**LAN**	*Línea Aérea Nacional de Chile*, also known as LAN Chile, the Chilean national civil airline
BAC	British Aircraft Corporation		**NCO**	Non-Commissioned Officer
BAM	*Base Aérea Militar*/Military Air Base (Argentina)		**OAS**	Organization of American States
BIPNA	*Batallón de Infantería de la Prefectura Naval Argentina*/Coast Guard Infantry Battalion (Argentina)		**PT Boat**	Patrol Torpedo boat
			TIAR	*Tratado Interamericano de Asistencia Recíproca*/Inter-American Treaty of Reciprocal Assistance
CASA	*Construcciones Aeronáuticas S.A.* (Spain)			
CATOS	*Comando Aéreo del Teatro de Operaciones Sur*/Theatre of Operations South Air Command (Argentina)		**UN**	United Nations
			VHF	Very High Frequency
FACh	*Fuerza Aérea de Chile*/Chilean Air Force		**YPF**	*Yacimientos Petrolíferos Fiscales*/Fiscal Oilfields (Argentina)
FLOMAR	*Flota del Mar*/Sea Fleet (Argentina)			
FMA	*Fábrica Militar de Aviones*/Military Aircraft Factory (Argentina)			

ACKNOWLEDGEMENTS

The author wishes to express his deep gratitude to Argentine Aviation historians Esteban Raczynski, Vladimiro Cettolo, Atilio Marino, Argentine Air Force Commodore (Ret.) Gabriel Pavlovcic, Argentine Air Force NCO (Ret.) Walter Marcelo Bentancor, the Chilean historian Claudio Cáceres Godoy, Michel Anciaux, Peruvian historian Amaru Tincopa, Archivo General de la Nación Argentina, Dirección de Estudios Históricos de la Fuerza Aérea Argentina, Museo Nacional de Aeronáutica de Argentina, Fuerza Aérea de Chile, Museo Nacional Aeronáutico y del Espacio de Chile, Archivo y Biblioteca Histórica de la Armada de Chile, for the invaluable data and photos for this volume.

INTRODUCTION

The Beagle Conflict reached its climax on 22 December 1978 when the Argentine Military Junta ordered *Operación Soberanía* (Operation Sovereignty): the invasion of the disputed islands, but retracting its execution when the clash between the Chilean Sea Squadron and the Argentine Sea Fleet was imminent. The last-minute political decision of the Argentine Military Junta to accept the Vatican's intervention prevented the imminent war.

The governments of Argentina and Chile agreed that the mediator should be the Pope, who sent Monsignor Antonio Samoré as his representative to mediate between the governments. On 12 December 1980, Pope John Paul II delivered a peace proposal to both governments.

The Papal proposals granted Chile the islands of Lennox, Picton, Nueva, Evout, Barnevelt, Freycinet, Wollaston, Terhalten and Sesambre, up to the island of Hornos. The surrounding line of the coasts of these islands constituted the so-called Chilean Territorial Sea, within which the Pope granted Argentina the possibility of installing navigation aids in the Evout and Barnevelt islands and a joint air terminal control system on New Island, in order to regulate flights to and from Antarctica. Likewise, the Vatican proposal established a Zone of Joint and Concerted Activities or Zone or Sea of Peace, where Argentina and Chile would jointly explore and exploit both the living and the non-living resources of the seabed and the subsoil.

While the Pinochet regime quickly accepted the Papal proposal, the Argentine military government delayed its response as long as it could, but finally communicated its rejection of the proposal. New incidents occurred on both sides, which served as justification for the abrupt Argentine decision to close the borders with Chile as a precautionary measure.

With the arrival of the hardliner Lieutenant General Leopoldo Galtieri to the Argentine presidency at the end of 1981, relations with Chile went through one of its most critical phases. The Beagle issue was perceived by the new President as the number one priority on the agenda. But the outbreak of the Falklands War between Argentina and the United Kingdom in April 1982 pushed the Beagle issue aside.

After the harsh defeat that Argentina received in the Falklands War, the first substantive agreement between the governments of Argentina and Chile was made on 15 September 1982, during the government of Lieutenant General Reynaldo Bignone. Both parties accepted the Vatican's invitation to extend the 1972 Treaty on the Judicial Settlement of Disputes. This agreement was due to the fact that neither of the two military regimes was willing to jeopardise the mediation, since both governments were facing serious internal crises. President Bignone and the members of the Argentine Military Junta decided to transfer the resolution of the problem to the future democratic government – which would take office in December 1983. Thus, on 26 July 1984, and before a definitive version of the agreement was reached, the democratic Argentine President Raúl Alfonsín convened a non-binding popular consultation.

The result of the Argentine popular consultation of 1984 was overwhelming: 82 percent of the population voted for the acceptance of the Papal proposal. Within this framework, the legislators accepted the signing of a peace treaty, and the signing of the Treaty of Peace and Friendship on 29 November 1984 ended the dispute over the Beagle Channel.

Chile obtained recognition of its sovereignty over all the islands south of Isla Grande de Tierra del Fuego (except the Argentine ones on the north side of the channel). In return, Chile renounced most of the marine rights that such islands grant under international law. In turn, both countries exchanged navigation rights in the area and Argentina renounced its aspirations in the Strait of Magellan.

1

THE HUGE MILITARY MOBILISATION IN BOTH COUNTRIES

In September 1978, the conflict with Chile over the sovereignty of the Beagle Channel Islands intensified. On 4 October, the Argentine authorities summoned the reservists under the slogan 'National Sovereignty, Priority Number One,' and all those who at that time were completing their compulsory military service were kept in their units. Incredibly, even the Bolivian Armed Forces were put on alert and deployed units to the border with Chile, 'for any eventuality.'

Both Chile and Argentina began deploying troops south by air, sea and land. In both countries the transport was carried out at night, so as not to alarm the civilian population. In the case of Chile, in addition to army and marine troops, around 9,000 carabineros were also deployed to reinforce the border checkpoints with Argentina. These carabineros had been trained in the infantry school of the Chilean Army. The Chilean Maritime Company, Empremar, provided the merchant ship *Lago Maihue* to the Chilean Army for the transfer of several regiments from the Maule and Bío-Bío regions to the Austral theatre of operations. By December, Chile had some 18,000 troops in the southern zone, but a total of 125,000 troops were mobilised in the whole country. Starting in October, all the units in the southern zone of Chile were reinforced. Thus, troops began to arrive from the Army regiments *Chacabuco*

and *Silva Renard* from Concepción, *Andalién* from Cauquenes, *Maipó* from Valparaíso and *Lautaro* from Rancagua, plus the entire

Three of the four Barceló-class PT Boats of the Chilean Navy, in a tactical camouflage scheme, patrolling the area of the southern canals at the end of 1978. (Esteban Raczynski Collection)

The merchant ship *Lago Maihue* of the private company Empremar was placed at the disposal of the Chilean Army for the transport of two regiments to the theatre of operations in the south. (Histarmar Archives)

The *Lanceros* Regiment of the Chilean Army deployed to the south in the Puerto Natales area in December 1978. (Ejército de Chile)

Crew of a Chilean Army M41 Walker Bulldog tank posing during manoeuvres in 1978 (left). Chilean Army soldiers receiving ammunition for their Mauser rifles during manoeuvres in southern Chile (right). (Ejército de Chile)

Troops from the *Caupolicán* Regiment of the Chilean Army posing with their Commanding Officer. (Ejército de Chile)

contingent that began their mandatory military service that year. Regarding the southern military units, the *Caupolicán* Regiment from Porvenir was to defend the Isla Grande de Tierra del Fuego, the *Pudeto* Regiment and the 5th Armoured Regiment would be in charge of defending Punta Arenas and the *Lanceros* Regiment of Puerto Natales. The Marine Infantry of the Chilean Navy (*Armada de Chile*, ACH) occupied the disputed islands and the Chilean Air Force (*Fuerza Aérea de Chile*, FACh) was in charge of protecting the airports of Puerto Natales, Punta Arenas and Porvenir, with control of the airspace in that region.

The High Command of the Chilean Army divided the country's territory into six defence areas, from north to south, with the VI Division in Iquique, the I Division in Antofagasta, the II Division in Santiago, the III Division in Valdivia, the IV Division in Coyhaique and the V Division in Punta Arenas.

On both sides of the border, troops from the two armies proceeded to build trenches and lay anti-personnel mines

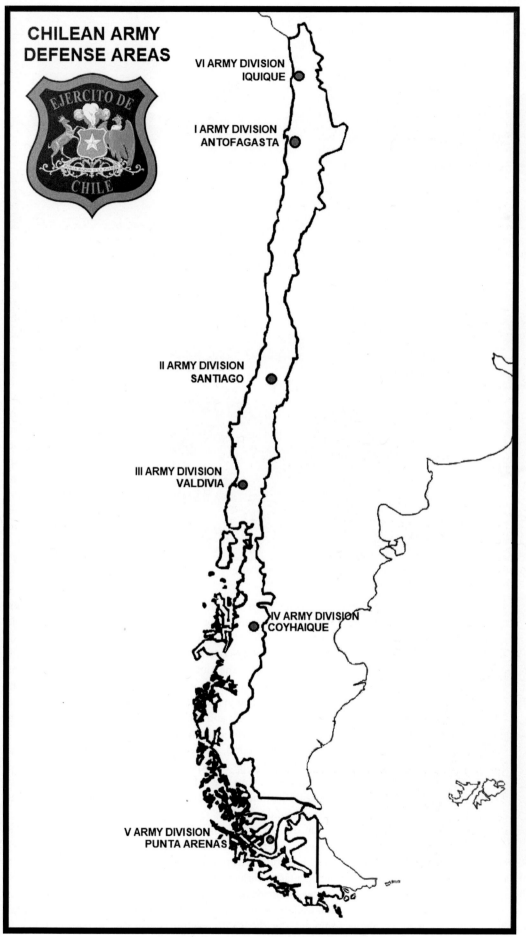

CHILEAN ARMY DEFENSE AREAS

EJERCITO DE CHILE

VI ARMY DIVISION
IQUIQUE

I ARMY DIVISION
ANTOFAGASTA

II ARMY DIVISION
SANTIAGO

III ARMY DIVISION
VALDIVIA

IV ARMY DIVISION
COYHAIQUE

V ARMY DIVISION
PUNTA ARENAS

Chilean Army Defence areas in 1978. (Map by the Author)

in places where invasion forces were likely to come through. In some cases, the advanced combat outposts of the two countries were less than 500 metres from each other. A tactical advantage that the Chileans possessed in the southern zone was that many of their reservist soldiers called up had worked in the mines in the Río Turbio and Río Gallegos areas in Argentine territory and knew the terrain very well.

Meanwhile, in Argentina, the Air Force's F-86F Sabre Squadron was again ordered to be reactivated. Captains Alberto A. Catalá and Luis A. Puga, who were in the A-4C Squadron, were also assigned to fly as Sabre test pilots and to collaborate with personnel from the Río IV Material Area in the commissioning of as many F-86Fs as possible. They recovered 13 aircraft, 100 percent of the aircraft in flying condition. They even upgraded all the aircraft's weapons by exchanging the six machine guns for new weapons found in their original containers in the Río Cuarto depots. As soon as they were ready, they transferred the Sabres to the IV Air Brigade. Brigadier José C. González Castro continued to lead the Brigade and Commodore Juan J. Ahets Etcheberry was appointed chief of Operations of Group 4.

In addition, thanks to a contract with the Chincul aircraft factory in San Juan, an operation was set up to replace the old communications and navigation systems on the Sabres. They were fitted with a multi-channel VHF radio, solid-state automatic direction finding, a low-priced but high-performance VHF omnidirectional range/instrument landing system, and a radio magnetic indication system. It turned out to be contradictory that, after long years of struggling with the old equipment and only months before the definitive

The North American F-86F Sabre fighters had been virtually retired from service, but due to the Beagle Crisis, they were 'dusted off' and fitted with new communication and navigation equipment. (Dirección de Estudios Históricos de la Fuerza Aérea Argentina)

A Douglas A-4B Skyhawk shares the platform with a North American F-86F Sabre at Río Gallegos Air Base in late 1978. (Vladimiro Cettolo Collection)

As of the end of October, the squadron was activated and the pilots summoned the previous year were recalled, as follows: Squadron Leader: Vice Commodore José A. Juliá, Crewmembers: Vice Commodores Héctor M. Sambrizzi, Carlos G. Velasco and Héctor R. Gilobert; Majors Luis J. Litrenta Carracedo, Rubén G. Zini, Saúl E. Costa and Amando N. Medina; Captain Baldomero A. Colom; First Lieutenants Miguel A. Alberto, Ricardo L. Altamirano and Osvaldo R. Battioni; Lieutenants Pablo A. Keppler, Carlos Kisiel, Jorge A. López and Roberto L. Yebra.

Like any other Argentine Air Force weapon system, the Sabre Squadron was enlisted for war. Due to the limited time available, experienced officers and non-commissioned officers were called in to keep the planes operational, train the crews, and prepare the support to deploy to the south. They came from various destinations: Senior Technician (R) Héctor C. Delgado, who was in charge of the Chincul-Piper plant in San Juan; retired non-commissioned officers residing in Mendoza; and those who were active, were assigned to the A-4C and MS.760 squadrons.

During this period, intense training activity was carried out for the pilots, including numerous maintenance flights and checks of the different systems which had been inactive for a long time. Once the rehabilitation was over, they went on to practice air-to-air and air-to-ground tactics.

On 12 December, the Sabre Squadron was deployed to Río Gallegos, after a technical stop in Trelew. In the following days, the pilots trained in reconnaissance, air defence and surface force support tasks. Perhaps the most significant event with these ageing fighters occurred on 19 December 1978 when six Sabres deployed in Río Gallegos entered Chilean airspace around Río Turbio. Some 18 minutes later, the F-86Fs reversed course when a confrontation with FACh Hunters seemed inevitable.

An Argentine Air Force pilot climbs into the cockpit of an F-86F Sabre fighter in the late 1970s. (Fernando Benedetto)

decommissioning, the Sabres were equipped with modern communication and navigation systems.

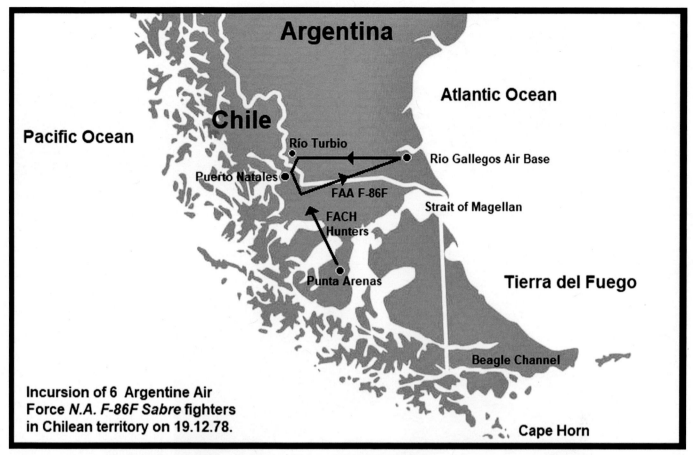

On 19 December 1978, six Argentine Air Force F-86F Sabre fighters made an incursion over Chilean territory for 18 minutes and then returned to their base in Río Gallegos. By the time the FACh Hawker Hunters arrived in the area, the Sabres had already left Chilean territory. (Map by author)

A formation of four Morane-Saulnier MS.760 Paris advanced trainers/light attack aircraft of the Argentine Air Force flying over the Andes. (Dirección de Estudios Históricos de la Fuerza Aérea Argentina)

On 5 September 1978, a squadron of Morane-Saulnier MS.760 Paris armed trainers, from the Air Force's Operational Squadron deployed to Río Gallegos in order to verify the operation at airfields set up on national routes near that city and Río Turbio. Between 16 and 20 October, and between 17 and 22 November, two squadrons were deployed again to Río Gallegos. They operated in the aerodromes located on the national routes. In addition, they carried out reconnaissance in the area. In compliance with Operations Order CATOS 78, the entire Operational Squadron was deployed to Río Gallegos where it continued its training in the area until 24 December.

Meanwhile, in 1978 Brigadier Antonio J. Crosetto was appointed brigade chief of the V Air Brigade and Commodore César A. Petre, chief of Operations Group 5. Vice commodore Héctor L. Destri and Major Arturo E. Pereyra commanded the air squadrons.

The squadrons of the 5th Fighter Group, which flew the Douglas A-4B Skyhawk attack aircraft, were formed by: Captains Carlos A. Morillo, César R. Magnano, Guillermo H. Brandi, Guillermo A. Donadille, Carlos A. Bunge, Jorge O. Fernández, Luis A. Vecchi and Guillermo O. Perondi; First Lieutenants Norberto R. Dimeglio, Higinio R. Robles, Jorge O. Ratti, José Treu, Héctor M. Benítez, Jorge L. Bergamaschi, Eduardo D. Almoño, Antonio F. Zelaya and Osvaldo Machinandiarena; Lieutenants Alberto J. Filippini, Oscar E. Berrier, Jorge D. Senn, Alejandro G. Brown, Daniel L. Herlein, Ernesto R. Ureta, Horacio H. Bosich, Marcelo E. Puig, Carlos M. Sellés, César F. Román, Carlos E. Perona, and the recent arrivals from the 2nd Fighter-Bomber Group (*Grupo de Caza Bombardero 2*, CB2): Lieutenants Luciano Guadagnini, Fausto Gavazzi Carlos E. Cachón and Juan C. Delgado and Ensigns Jorge M. Reta, Raúl A. Federico, José L. Ardiles, Mario M. Callejo, Ángel M. Villamil, Carlos A. Antonietti,

(Left) A Morane-Saulnier MS.760 Paris with a display of all of the types of weapons it could carry for close air support missions, at El Plumerillo Air Base in Mendoza. Note the F-86F Sabre fighters in the background near the hangars (upper left). (Right) An underwing machine gun pod and a 50kg bomb on a pylon. (Dirección de Estudios Históricos de la Fuerza Aérea Argentina)

Impressive flight line of Douglas A-4B Skyhawk aircraft of the 5th Fighter Group at Villa Reynolds, San Luis. (Dirección de Estudios Históricos de la Fuerza Aérea Argentina)

Thus began a long and tense wait where false alarms, as well as real ones, were not lacking.

In that tense December, the last activity of Operations Group 5 was the test of three different types of retarded bombs. Two of them, developed by the armament factory, were based on the operating principles of the British 500 kilogramme MK.17, supplied for the Canberra bombers; the third, a 250 kilogramme BRP19 without a fuse, which was in the process of being purchased from Alaveses, based in Spain. The test drops were made next to runway 05, in front of the flight tower of V Air Brigade.

A good number of the Argentine Air Force's fleet of helicopters were deployed to the then recently created Río Mayo Military Air Base in Chubut, including Bell 212s, Sikorsky S-61s and Hughes 369/500s for close air support to ground troops.

In 1978 Brigadier José C. González Castro was the commander of IV Air Brigade and its Douglas A-4C Skyhawks. Commodore Juan J. Ahets Etcheberry was appointed Chief of Operations Group 4 and Vice Commodore Juan Manuel Correa Cuenca, Chief of the A-4C Squadron.

The squadrons were made up of Captains Carlos A. Oliva, Gilberto H. Oliva, Gustavo A. Piuma Justo, Alfonso Ruggiero, Alberto A. Catalá, Carlos A. Morillo, Alberto Kajihara, Luis A. Puga and Fernando A. Castellano; First Lieutenants Jorge A. Pierini, Carlos A. Maffeis, Carlos A. Musso, Jorge R. Gatti, Jorge O. García, Jorge C. Dellepiane, Luis A. Demierre, and Carlos A. Moreno; and Lieutenant José D. Vazquez. Also flying in the squadron were Brigadier González Castro, Commodore Ahets Etcheberry, Majors Raúl Quiroga, Jorge G. Recalde, Joaquín P. Solaberrieta and Norberto I. Razquín, Captain Jorge E. Baravalle, First Lieutenants Guillermo R. Siri and Mario J. Caffaratti and Lieutenants Álvaro L. Pérez, Mariano A. Velasco, Normando Costantino, José L. Gabari Zoco and Eduardo González.

Danilo R. Bolzán and Héctor H. Sánchez. Brigadier Crosetto, Vice Commodore Alberto Alegría, Captains Nelson H. Godoy and Carlos A. Tomba, and First Lieutenant Germán E. Spika.

On 26 June, Commodore Aníbal A. Laborda assumed command of Operations Group 5. On 13 December, it was ordered that the operational strategic commands be constituted. Several former A-4 pilots, including Majors Oscar L. Aranda Durañona, Manuel A. Mariel, Raúl E. Echenique, Carlos A. Oliva and Daniel R. Otero, were recalled and joined the operational squadrons. The Strategic Air Command, to which the A-4Bs were assigned, ordered the Preventive Withdrawal of Phase 1 Enlistment. During the month of December 1978, the 1st Squadron of Operations Group 5 was deployed to the Naval Air Base Comandante Espora, which after the first combat mission would operate from Neuquén airport, and the 2nd Squadron to VII Air Brigade in Morón, and after the first mission it would withdraw and operate from V Air Brigade.

With the corresponding location of surveillance radars and deployment on the ground of the Air Observer Network, the Air Defence Sectors were organised. The defence of the most important objectives was covered with the scarce anti-aircraft artillery available and with the armed interceptors that remained on alert at each base.

Two Argentine Air Force Hughes 369 helicopters armed with rocket launchers. (José Ochoa via Comodoro (Ret.) Gabriel Pavlovcic)

A Bell 212 helicopter of the Argentine Air Force during the Antarctic Campaign in the late 1970s. (J. Figari via Comodoro Gabriel Pavlovcic)

A Morane-Saulnier MS.760 Paris and a Douglas A-4C Skyhawk of the Argentine Air Force. (SOP (Ret.) Walter Bentancor)

Las Lajas Shooting Range and the squadrons operating from Mendoza. For 30 minutes, 44 planes continuously fired cannons, bombs and rockets, in the presence of the highest national authorities.

On 5 September, a squadron was deployed to Río Gallegos in compliance with an operation ordered by the Air Operations Command.

On 10 October, operating from the Comandante Espora Naval Air Base, with the support of the Navy, Vice Commodore Correa Cuenca and Lieutenant Pérez tested the Israeli Shafrir air-to-air missiles fired from the A-4Cs, with satisfactory results.

Between 15 and 19 October, in order to carry out verification flights, the A-4C Airmobile Squadron was ordered to carry out a reduced deployment to the campaign aerodrome set up by the unit at the San Julián airport. The weapons configurations foreseen in

As part of the enlistment tasks before a possible armed confrontation with Chile, and with the double purpose of checking the weapons and showing both the domestic and the foreign public the operational level reached by the Air Force, the Operations Command ordered Operations Group IV to organise, coordinate and conduct a firepower demonstration on 10 May 1978. All combat units participated, with weapons used against targets built at the

the war plans were tested, acquiring, for the first time, real experience in these operations. At the end of October, relations with Chile became tense and enlistment measures increased. On 1 November, the A-4C Airmobile Squadron was officially created. On the 8th, training was accelerated to reach maximum operational capacity.

Captain Gustavo Piuma Justo, Head of Squadron Operations, recalled the following years later:

In the first days of November, the story spread that two F-5s of the Chilean Air Force (FACh), which had their base in Pudahuel (Santiago), on a high-altitude night flight had flown over Argentine territory, up to the Federal Capital and returned to their country. The Chilean officers had celebrated this feat with bottles of champagne and, with great pride, had boasted that they had touched us.... they had wet our ears. In the IV Brigade there were many officers since the Air Group was made up of a squadron of A-4Cs, another of F-86s, two of MS.760s and another of Lama helicopters.

(Left) Douglas A-4C Skyhawks of the Argentine Air Force at San Julián Air Base. (Right) Ground personnel preparing two Israeli Shafrir missiles to be mounted on an A-4C. (Via Vladimiro Cettolo & Dirección de Estudios Históricos de la Fuerza Aérea Argentina)

In the foreground, an Argentine Air Force Douglas A-4C Skyhawk with a display of the variety of the weapons it could carry, including different types of bombs, rocket launchers, fuel drop tanks, and even air-to-air missiles. In the background, an A-4B flight line. (Dirección de Estudios Históricos de la Fuerza Aérea Argentina)

The young men who were training for war and commented indignantly how no one had come out to intercept them. Obviously, it was impossible because we lacked radars in the area. The following week, another version circulated about a squadron of A-37s that, during daytime flight, had carried out a simulated attack on the San Rafael airfield. In my private heart I felt humiliated; I couldn't believe that these gentlemen would dare such audacity. One fine day, with less than 15 days to be

deployed to San Julián, I had an idea while having breakfast with my squad in the bar of the famous Fighter Group 1. We went to a classroom for the pre-flight briefing. The topic to be analysed was high-low-high navigation with an attack on a bridge in Neuquén; the day before we had prepared it. There, meeting with First Lieutenant Jorge Dellepiane, Captain Luis Puga (section chief) and Lieutenant Eduardo González – a.k.a. "Pata de lana" (wool leg), the newest of the Squadron – I announced to them that the flight was going to be very particular, that I needed a pledge of honour, and that I assumed full responsibility for this gentlemen's

(Left) Captain Gustavo Piuma Justo. (Centre) Douglas A-4C Skyhawk flight line. (Right) A section of Argentine Air Force A-4C aircraft, crewed by Captains Piuma and Puga, 1st Lieutenant Dellepiane and Lieutenant González, carried out a flight over Chilean territory in mid-November 1978. (Dirección de Estudios Históricos de la Fuerza Aérea Argentina. Map by author)

agreement; in return, I promised to baptise them on the waters of the Pacific.

Our call sign was "*Grillo*" [Cricket]. We left in the Bravo + 50 version, enough to fly for more than two hours. We took off heading south and climbed to level 260, lying on the edge, until I saw the Maipó volcano. We turned west and began to lose height. I ordered a tactical stagger to the left, and we descended following the profile of the mountain range, always heading for that mountain; it was a clear day. We continue to the west close to the ground. Already in the plain, I saw a city to the right and to my left, an airport and several planes on the platform, it was Temuco. We changed course to the Southwest until, suddenly, the great Pacific Ocean appeared. On its waters we turned north, parallel to and a mile from the coast, skimming the waves, for about 35 to 40 minutes. At first I only saw small towns. Suddenly, to the right, a major port and buildings appeared. Without having foreseen it, we were blocking Valparaíso, then Viña del Mar and the typical coastal buildings.

I admit that unconsciousness scared me. Anyway, we continued north until, through some extensive beaches, I assumed that we were in La Serena, a side of San Juan. So we headed east, entered the Continent and when crossing the Pan-American highway, I saw a column of trucks and armoured vehicles heading south. There I broke the silence and ordered: "Attack the armoured column," obviously simulated. In the first passage, I observed that the troops greeted us, convinced that we were Chilean.

Encouraged, I ordered "Reemploy!" At the end, I began to gain height with the staggered squadron to the left. I knew that the only Chilean radar was the one in Pudahuel and, if they intercepted us, they would come from the right. When we were already lined up and close to the border, it occurred to me to play a prank on my squad and shouted: "Bandits at 6!" which is the position that requires you to turn your head as much as possible. That was when the 4, "Pata de lana", exclaimed, with an anguished voice: "Look, there are two!" The spread that was armed was unimaginable. Each one gave full engine trying to cross the border as soon as possible. Thus, it was that I informed the Tower that the Grillo Squadron would make an individual landing.

The next day, the Squad met in the classroom and we toasted with champagne. I remember telling them that while this flight was a ride, we could also do it with weapons…[1]

On 19 November, Operations Order CATOS 78 came into effect. The A-4C Airmobile Squadron was deployed to the south: three squadrons to San Julián and one to Comodoro Rivadavia. During the month of November, a LAN Chile (*Línea Aérea Nacional de Chile*) Boeing 707 violated Argentine airspace and was intercepted by an Air Force A-4C armed with Shafrir air-to-air missiles, forcing it to leave the area. On the 29th, the Commander-in-Chief of the Air Force, Brigadier General Orlando R. Agosti, inspected the unit. On 19 December, the transfer of the squadron to San Julián was completed. At that base, an electronics workshop was set up, and the AWE-1 firing programmers were put into service in all the planes.

Chilean photographic reconnaissance flights had been detected and the A-4C Squadron was ordered to intercept them. On one occasion, they crossed the vertical of San Julián and the alert section took off. The A-4C pilots were able to see a FACh Learjet which, knowing that it was being pursued, escaped at full power heading west. At top speed, the A-4Cs could not intercept it.

On 22 December, the Argentine command needed to discover the response capacity of the FACh's air defences and a mission was ordered to test it. Around 10 pm, a section of A-4Cs took off, made up of Captain Piuma and Lieutenant González, in the Charlie version, to fly over Punta Arenas and observe the reaction of the

In November 1978, a LAN Chile Boeing 707 (left) violated Argentine airspace, apparently without communication with air traffic controllers. Immediately, an Argentine Air Force A-4C Skyhawk with Shafrir missiles (right) took off and intercepted the Chilean jetliner, forcing it to leave Argentine airspace. (Museo Nacional de Aeronáutica y Espacio de Chile & Dirección de Estudios Históricos de la Fuerza Aérea Argentina)

Left) Flight line of the Douglas A-4B Skyhawks of the 5th Fighter Group (C-5) at Villa Reynolds, V Air Brigade. (right) Bomb-armed Douglas A-4C Skyhawks from the 4th Fighter Group (C-4) at El Plumerillo, IV Air Brigade. (SOP (Ret) Walter Bentancor)

Maintenance personnel from the Argentine Air Force posing next to a Dassault Mirage IIIEA fighter. (SOP (Ret.) Walter Bentancor)

(Left) A Dassault Mirage IIIEA in Mendoza in 1978. A pair of Bell 212 helicopters and a Sikorsky S-61 can be seen in the background. (Right) An AMD-BA Mirage IIIDA of the Argentine Air Force. (Via Vladimiro Cettolo)

enemy fighters. The operation was carried out with the support of the Río Gallegos Information and Control Centre (CIC) radar. After reaching 10,000 feet, the expected flight level, the A-4C leader found that the heating was not working and that his feet were almost frozen. Despite this, they continued and the radar guided them over Punta Arenas. Suddenly, with an alarmed tone, the radar controller warned them to make a 180° turn and return to Argentine territory, because two F-5s had just taken off. On the way back, the A-4Cs flew over Río Gallegos and Puerto Santa Cruz. The flight became long and exhausting. The weather worsened, it began to rain and González was left without a radio. Through hand signs, the No.2 informed Piuma Justo that he was losing fuel. As the last section of the flight was over the sea, the prospect was alarming but they arrived in San Julián safely.

Two days after this episode, Chile and Argentina accepted Papal mediation. Command ordered the withdrawal of most of the aircraft but, as a precaution, a precautionary deployment of the weapons systems most exposed to a surprise attack was maintained, among them, the A-4C Squadron, which was redeployed to the Río IV Material Area, on 27 December.

The dispute with Chile over the islands of the Beagle Channel involved VIII Air Brigade at Mariano Moreno Air Base, in the province of Buenos Aires, in the Air Force's first real preparation for war, and had to deploy a Mirage IIIEA squadron to the south of the country. The unit was also charged with the responsibility of receiving and putting into operational service the Israel Aircraft Industries (IAI) M5 Daggers, which were purchased from Israel to reinforce the ground attack capability of the A-4B Skyhawk.

On 8 December, as part of the Operations Plan, the deployment of a reduced squadron of Mirage IIIs to IX Air Brigade, in Comodoro Rivadavia, was ordered to integrate the air resources of the Air Command of the South Theatre of Operations (*Comando Aéreo del Teatro de Operaciones Sur*, CATOS). The squadron had the mission of providing air cover for the ground operations planned for the recovery of the disputed island, and as a secondary task, the air defence of BAM (*Base Aérea Militar*, Military Air Base) Río Gallegos and other objectives of the Southern Theatre of Operations (*Teatro de Operaciones Sur*, TOS). In total, five Mirage IIIEAs and one IIIDA were deployed there, each one carrying a Matra 530 missile on the ventral pylon. The squadron would remain in Comodoro Rivadavia until they were ordered to redeploy to Río Gallegos, around 23 December.

That day, Major Villar, at the head of the squadron, with the squadron leaders, Major Eduardo R. Costa and Captain Julio C.

The first batch of IAI M5 Dagger (Nesher) fighter-bombers purchased by the Argentine Air Force being prepared for shipment. (Atilio Marino via Vladimiro Cettolo)

Farkas, the section chiefs, Captains Mario A. Demartini and Juan E. Scherer, and the wingmen, Captain Carlos A. Luna and First Lieutenant Jorge A. Testa, with one two-seater and five single-seat Mirage IIIs, took off bound for Comodoro Rivadavia. The jets were configured with two 1,700-litre fuel tanks and a Matra 530 missile each. The Mirage III Squadron based in Comodoro Rivadavia carried out training and reconnaissance missions in the area of operations. On several occasions, it flew over Balmaceda and Puerto Aysén, in Chilean territory.

In mid-December, three additional Mirage IIIs flew to Río Gallegos to reinforce the first six and to relieve crews. For days, they trained conscientiously until, on 23

IAI M5 Dagger fighter-bombers of the Argentine Air Force. (Dirección de Estudios Históricos de la Fuerza Aérea Argentina)

December they received the order to move to Río Gallegos and there configure the planes with cannons and bombs in order to attack a Chilean objective at first light of the next day. However, that evening, after landing at Río Gallegos, there was news to surprise and relieve the staff: operations were suspended and the return to the units of origin on 24 December was ordered by decision of the President of the Nation upon accepting the Papal mediation offered by Cardinal Samoré.

The first IAI M5 Dagger fighter-bombers arrived at the port of Buenos Aires in late November 1978. Captains Julio C. Farkas and Carlos F. Neme were responsible for receiving them at the docks and supervising the land transfer to the hangar of *Austral Líneas Aéreas*, at Jorge Newbery Airport; the transfer was made at night under strict security and concealment conditions. At Jorge Newbery, with the assistance of Israel Aircraft Industries technicians, they were made airworthy. The first 26 Daggers arrived in three batches of six and a fourth batch of eight.

The purchase contract for US$109,102,000, that included the acquisition of 24 single-seaters and a pair of two-seater fighters was signed on 10 August 1978. All IAI M5 Nesher fighters were to be inspected and their systems updated. Ground support equipment

and 50 Shafrir missiles were also purchased. This purchase was carried out in the utmost secrecy and in the shortest time possible. These planes acquired the name *Dagger*, which was also the code name for the purchase project. In order to speed up the process of receiving and adapting to the new aircraft, it was decided that the pilots should receive training in different places, such as in the VIII Brigade with the Mirage IIIEA of the 8th Fighter Group, and also at Captain Quiñones González Air Force Base of the Peruvian Air Force (*Fuerza Aérea del Perú*) in Chiclayo, within the 611th Fighter squadron, which was equipped with Mirage 5P/DP aircraft. The rest of the personnel, some 12 officers and 32 non-commissioned officers, were sent to Israel in October, to the Negev Squadron at Eitam Air Base in the Sinai, to be trained by the Israeli Air Force. Eight Argentine pilots took the flight course, using only Argentine aircraft and not wearing any type of insignia, since the entire operation was secret. The Argentine pilots trained in Israel were Major Sapolski, Captains Pergolini, Donadille, Kahijara, Martínez and Puga, First Lieutenants Arnau and Mir González, Almoño, DiMeglio, Janet and Musso. Maintenance personnel were trained by IAI at Ben Gurion International Airport in Lod.

Some Argentine Air Force pilots at Eitam Air Base of the Israeli Air Force posing with an IAI Nesher during their secret training. The photo was taken on 28 November 1978. From left to right, Captains Alberto Kajihara, Carlos Martínez and Luis Puga, First Lieutenants Eduardo Almoño, Robert Janet and Carlos Musso. (Dirección de Estudios Históricos de la Fuerza Aérea Argentina)

The initial decision regarding where to keep the Daggers until the adaptation of the Tandil Military Air Base was to base them at Mariano Moreno and the Dagger Squadron remained operating in that Air Brigade until the Strategic Air Command ordered its transfer to its operational deployment base in the Río IV Material Area on 8 December 1978. At the end of that month, after the deflation of the conflict with Chile, the initial decision was revoked and it was decided to keep the squadron operating in the Material Area temporarily until its definitive location in Tandil.

On the same date as the Mirage IIIEAs, 8 December, a squadron of six M5 Daggers, assigned to the Strategic Air Command and configured as an airmobile squadron, was deployed to the Río IV Material Area together with their technical support, with the task of training with the material just received and preparation to go into operations from that relative position. Fragmentary orders for the squadron's first sorties encompassed air-to-ground attacks on assigned material targets. As a secondary task, it had to carry out the air defence of the Material Area, for which it was planned there would be aircraft on daytime alert on the ground armed with guns and Shafrir missiles. This squadron was made up of Major Mario E. Román as chief, as Squadron leaders Major Juan C. Sapolski and Captain Héctor M. Pergolini, as section chiefs the first lieutenants

Carlos A. Arnau and Horacio Mir González, and as squadron officer, First Lieutenant Amílcar G. Cimatti. On 20 December, the squadron was completed with the pilots who received training in Israel.

The locally manufactured FMA (*Fábrica Militar de Aviones/ Military Aircraft Factory*) IA.58 Pucará attack aircraft were based at Reconquista Military Air Base. The name *Pucará* was a Quechua language word meaning fortress. The tension with Chile over the border issue increased and led to a series of actions. It was necessary to increase the crews, according to the numbers calculated by the Planning Factor Tables (TFP), and in November 1978, the directive that contemplated the mobilisation of the Pucará aircraft towards the alternative bases was finished, in anticipation of future actions. One of the most common anticipated actions consisted of the flight of a squadron (usually four planes) to the IV Air Brigade, where it was separated into two sections. One flew along the Andes to Ushuaia to the south and the other, to the north, to Jujuy. The aircraft would operate autonomously and the pilots acquired adequate preparation to act in areas of difficult access and without ground support.

The Operations Plan of Command for a possible conflict with Chile due to border issues included the transfer of all the IA.58 aircraft to the province of Santa Cruz. In order to carry out an effective test of the response capacity, the 3rd Attack Squadron began a series of trips to the south that year to establish the future operating conditions at those bases. The first began on 7 November, with the squadron leader, Vice Commodore Ignes Rosset, heading to the San Julián aerodrome and returned to Reconquista two days later. On the 19th, a mobile squadron departed to San Julián and landed in Comodoro Rivadavia. The next day, it took off for Santa Cruz and Río Gallegos. On 21 November, it moved to Gobernador Gregores, returning to Río Gallegos on the same day; and on the 22nd, another flight to Santa Cruz. On the 24th, it arrived in Reconquista.

The first deployments were carried out in December, when the support planes began to transfer personnel and materials to the airfields foreseen in the planning. For this operation, the IA.58s would be assisted by an *Fábrica Militar de Aviones* technical team, with logistical support from the Military Aviation School.

The first Pucará Squadron left on 20 December for the Puerto de Santa Cruz Military Air Base, located in the town of the same name, about 200 kilometres north of Río Gallegos. Commanded by Vice Commodore Ignes Rosset, it was made up of Captain Kettle, First Lieutenants Palaver, Varela and Filippi; Lieutenants

FMA IA.58 Pucará attack aircraft deployed in the area of Puerto Santa Cruz, in southern Argentina, operating from national roads in November 1978. (Via Vladimiro Cettolo)

The all-terrain capability of the Pucará attack aircraft made it possible to operate even from unpaved roads in southern Argentina during the Beagle Crisis at the end of 1978. (Vladimiro Cettolo Collection)

Ballesteros, Cáceres, Navarro, Raffaini, Bustos and Brunacci; and Ensigns Gismondi and Cordini Brunner. They were also accompanied by First Lieutenant Spika of the Flight Test Centre (*Centro de Entrenamiento de Vuelo*, CEV). The aircraft serials were A-511, A-512, A-514, A-516, A-520 and A-522.

The second squadron, under the command of Vice Commodore Carbó Bernard, took off the same day towards the Fort General Roca Military Air Base, in the city of the same name, located in the northwest of Río Negro. It was formed with the Captains Igarzábal and Bonavía; First Lieutenants Benítez, Vila, Grünert, Bacarezza, and Rodino; Lieutenants Fasani and Federici; and Ensigns Russo, Hernández and Braun; it was completed with Major Digier, Captain Carlos A. Tomba and First Lieutenant Rogelio R. Marzialetti of CEV. The aircraft serials were AX-04, A-507, A-509, A-510, A-513, A-515, A-517 and A-523.

As with other squadrons, the moment of greatest tension was experienced on 22 December, when the order to start operations was received, but when the pilots and their

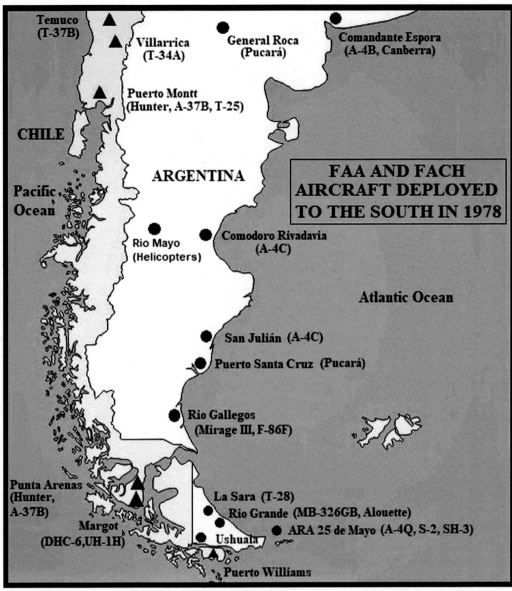

The map shows the tactical deployment of combat aircraft of the Chilean Air Force and the Argentine Air Force to the south, during the Beagle Conflict at the end of 1978. (Map by author)

aircraft were ready for take-off, the order was cancelled. The intervention of Pope John Paul II's envoy, Cardinal Antonio Samoré, had borne fruit: the governments of both countries agreed to stop their actions and begin negotiations. With that situation overcome, the withdrawal of the Pucará squadrons began on the same day.

Meanwhile, at the beginning of December in Puerto Belgrano, the Argentine fleet weighed anchor to begin its journey south. Several kilometres to the north, the Mar del Plata Submarine Base

was also immersed in great activity. Under the watchful eye of senior naval officers, military personnel from the unit worked feverishly on final details. When everything was ready, the order to start was given and, as if in slow motion, the four boats of the Submarine Force separated from the docks to slowly head towards the exit, firstly the modern German-built IKL-209 ARA *San Luis* (S-32) and ARA *Salta* (S-31), under the command of the Frigate Captains Félix Rodolfo Bartolomé and Eulogio Moya respectively, followed by the

Left) The Argentine Navy Submarine Force Command building. (Right) The submarine S-22 ARA *Santiago del Estero* at its base in Mar del Plata. (Histarmar Archives)

(Left) General Prefects Alberto Mancinelli and Alberto Mancuso, during the inspection of the PNA (*Prefectura Naval Argentina*/Argentine Coast Guard) Air Group at Cabo Domingo Auxiliary Aerodrome. A Coast Guard Hughes 369 helicopter can be seen in the background. (Right) Commander of the Marine Infantry, Rear Admiral Oscar Francisco Abriata (front right) greeting the BIPNA Albatross troops. To his right is the battalion's commander, Senior Prefect Rubén Omar Williams, along with other senior Coast Guard officers. (Prefectura Naval Argentina)

veteran Guppy ARA *Santa Fe* (S-21) and ARA *Santiago del Estero* (S-22) under the orders of Frigate Captains Alberto R. Manfrino and Carlos Sala.

The Marine Infantry Command (COIM) deployed seven battalions of Marines to the south, to which was added an infantry battalion from the Argentine Naval Prefecture (*Batallón de Infantería de la Prefectura Naval Argentina*, BIPNA), known as the Albatross Battalion, the latter made up of five companies of riflemen, one commando and another for services, with a total of 445 effectives, as part of *Operación Nubarrón* (Operation Dark Cloud). The Argentine Coast Guard also mobilised an Air Group made up of Short Skyvan aircraft and Hughes 369 helicopters that operated under the Naval Aviation Command (*Comando de la Aviación Naval*, COAN), based in the Río Grande Naval Air Base in Tierra del Fuego. The BIPNA troops were assigned to urban defence in the Ushuaia area and the Air Group aircraft for liaison and reconnaissance tasks in the Beagle area.

Days before, the Chilean squadron had also sailed from the Talcahuano Naval Base, led by its flagship, the cruiser ACH *Pratt* under the command of Ship Captain Eri Solís Oyarzún, with the commander of the fleet, Vice Admiral Raúl López Silva on board; the destroyers ACH *Almirante Williams* (Captain Ramón Undurraga Carvajal) and ACH *Almirante Riveros* (Captain Huber Von Apeen), the frigates ACH *Almirante Lynch* (Captain Humberto Ramírez Olivari) and ACH *Condell* (Frigate Captain Erwin Conn Tesche), the destroyers ACH *Zenteno* (Frigate Captain Arturo García Petersen), ACH *Portales* (Navy Captain Mariano Sepúlveda Matus), ACH *Cochrane* (Navy Captain Carlos Aguirre Vidaurre Leal) and ACH *Blanco Encalada* (Frigate Captain Jorge Fellay Fuenzalida), in addition to the oil tanker ACH *Araucano* (Captain Jorge Grez Casarino), the logistics vessel ACH *Yelcho* (Lieutenant Commander Gustavo Marín Watkins), the ACH *Aldea* (Lieutenant Commander Octavio Bolelli Luna), the ACH *Lientur* (Lieutenant Commander Ariel Rozas Mascaró), the ACH *Beagle* (Lieutenant Commander Sergio del Campo Santelices) and the aged submarine ACH *Simpson* (Lieutenant Rubén Scheihing Navarro). There were a total of 4,000 crew members with 200 officers embarked.

The cruiser ACH *Latorre* (Navy Captain Sergio Sánchez Luna) joined the squadron later, since its departure was delayed due to being under repair. Another warship that was left behind was the cruiser ACH *O'Higgins* (Navy Captain Eduardo Angulo), also under repair, but it was not moved to the south and remained in Talcahuano Naval Base for local defence.

The fleet headed for Tierra del Fuego and the Beagle Channel, with instructions to meet with the support units subordinated to the Third Naval Zone under the command of Rear Admiral Luis de los Ríos Echeverría, namely, the ACH *Serrano* (Frigate Captain Rodolfo Calderón Aldunate), the ACH *Uribe* (Frigate Captain Adolfo Carrasco Lagos), the ACH *Orella* (Frigate Captain Raúl Manríquez Lagos), the Landing Ship (Tank) ACH *Araya* (Frigate Captain Gastón Silva Cañas), the ACH *Colo Colo* (Corvette Captain Sergio del Campo Santelices) and ACH *Piloto Pardo* (Frigate Captain Gustavo Pfeifer Niedbalski). During the voyage to the south, the crews of the ships in the squadron, in addition to carrying out combat practices, also dedicated themselves to carrying out painting tasks to camouflage the ships.

The submarine force was under the command of Rear Admiral Osvaldo Schwarzemberg Stegmaier and although it had four boats, it

The three light cruisers of the Chilean Navy in war colour schemes. From left to right, ACH *Almirante Latorre* (CL-4), ACH *O'Higgins* (CL-2), and ACH *Capitán Prat* (CL-3). (Archivo Histórico de la Armada de Chile)

The Chilean Navy frigate ACH *Almirante Lynch*, with an Alouette III helicopter on its flight deck and the Exocet missile launchers on the stern, seen on 19 December 1978. (Museo Naval y Marítimo de Valparaíso)

The Chilean Navy Destroyer DD-15 ACH *Cochrane* (DD-15), in its wartime colour scheme, in 1978. (Archivo Histórico de la Armada de Chile)

The Destroyers ACH *Ministro Portales* (DD-17) (left), and ACH *Almirante Williams* (DDG-19) (right), of the Chilean Navy. (Archivo Histórico de la Armada de Chile)

could only deploy one, the aforementioned ACH *Simpson*. Its twin, ACH *Thomson*, was under repair during the crisis, ACH *O'Brien* (Frigate Captain Juan Mackay Barriga) had to go in to dock for maintenance and ACH *Hyatt* (Frigate Captain Ricardo Kompatzki Contreras) had to return to Talcahuano due to serious failures in its propulsion systems.

Chile hoped to make up for these shortcomings with the Naval Aviation, which only had air-maritime exploration means that arrived in the country in the last months of the year and the helicopters embarked in some of the Sea Squadron vessels, all under the command of Captain Sergio Mendoza Rojas, supported by Claudio Aguayo Herrera, in charge of the air naval resources of the southern zone and those of the air under the command of Lieutenant

The only operational submarine of the Chilean Navy, ACH *Simpson* (SS-21), next to the polar ship ACH *Piloto Pardo* (AP-45), in southern Chile in 1978. (Archivo Histórico de la Armada de Chile)

Commander René Maldonado Bouchon. In fact, the commander of the Sea Squadron, Vice Admiral López, had been a naval aviator and gave great importance to Naval Aviation, since it had to follow the movements of the Argentine Sea Fleet to prevent surprise attacks.

The Marine Infantry forces, for their part, had their forts in the Miller and Cochrane detachments, in the Marine Infantry School and other smaller units, all of them under the command of Rear Admiral IM (*Infantería de Marina*, Marine Infantry) Sergio Cid Araya with Captain IM Pablo Wunderlich Piderit as his deputy, in

charge of an operational support brigade – very little to face the enemy Naval Aviation that could operate from nearby airports and airfields and from the aircraft carrier ARA *Veinticinco de Mayo*.

The difference between the two sides was huge in terms of aviation, since the Argentine Air Force had 44 operational A-4B Skyhawk attack aircraft out of the 50 acquired in 1966 and 25 A-4C purchased in 1975. Most of the Argentine fighters were concentrated in the 4th and 5th Fighter Groups, the first, a component of the IV Air Brigade based in El Plumerillo, Mendoza, and the second, of the V Air Brigade in Villa Reynolds, San Luis. The 4th Fighter Group had deployed its aircraft and the maintenance plant to a base in the south, possibly San Julián, where the 6th Fighter Group of Tandil would also operate.

By this time, Argentina had Westinghouse AN-TPS43 and W-430 mobile type radar systems which had been incorporated into the Air Force in October 1978. For this reason, a special squadron was created, dependent on Air Surveillance School Group 1 (GIVA-E).

On 2 December, Brigadier Gilberto Hilario Oliva had issued a call to all pilots in Argentina to go to their nearest bases and get ready to defend the nation's sovereignty. The idea was to create a structure made up of civilian aviators aimed at covering and reinforcing the operational needs of the Air Force in times of war. This would allow the creation of an already trained team, capable of different degrees of scope, utility and complexity, to respond to the varied military requirements according to the type of task that had to be faced. This is how the *Escuadrón Fénix* (Phoenix Squadron) was created, which had a crucial role during the Falklands War of 1982. Retired Captain Jorge Luis Páez Allende was summoned, who began with the organisational tasks necessary to constitute such a squadron. On that occasion, it was possible to have a significant number of aircraft and another considerable number of pilots and aircraft mechanics. This tactical/strategic use would allow a strong impact on the possible opponent, generating a strong psychological pressure on the enemy's defence lines.

The *Escuadrón Fénix* made up of civil aviators had Lear Jet LR-24, LR-25, LR-35, Cessna Citation C-500, Hawker Siddeley HS-125, BAC 1-11 jets, Turbo Commander AC690, Mitsubishi MU-2, FMA IA.50G2 Guaraní, Merlín III-B turboprop aircraft, Aerocommander AC50, Grand-Commander AC68, Aerostar TS600, TS601, Douglas DC-3, C-47 piston aircraft, and turbine helicopters such as Augusta 109A, Bell 212, 205-A1, 206, Bolkow BO-105, Hughes 500, Sikorsky S-58ET and S-61N.

Faced with such strength, the Chileans saw with anguish the crystallisation of the conflict, but they placed their trust in the intervention of the Holy Father, who they knew would end up understanding the magnitude of the problem and ruling in

Aerospatiale SA.319B Alouette III helicopters of the Chilean Naval Aviation on board the ships of the Sea Squadron in 1978. (Archivo Histórico de la Armada de Chile)

By 1978, the Argentine Air Force had 44 A-4B Skyhawks still in service of the 50 purchased in 1966, and 25 A-4Cs purchased in 1975. (Dirección de Estudios Históricos de la Fuerza Aérea Argentina)

Westinghouse AN/TPS-43 radar of the Argentine Air Force. (Dirección de Estudios Históricos de la Fuerza Aérea Argentina)

A FACh Northrop F-5E Tiger II (above) and a F-5F (below). (FACh via Claudio Cáceres Godoy)

their favour, avoiding war. Supporting Chile meant respecting international law and the arbitration ruling against the brute force that Argentina was willing to use.

According to *Radio Iquique*, at 07:40 a.m. a FACh Northrop F-5E Tiger II piloted by Lieutenant Hernán Gabrielli detected the passage of two Argentine planes that were flying very close to the Tacora volcano, violating Chilean airspace. The story was never confirmed and was no more than a rumour, one of the many that circulated in those days, but it left a marked sense of concern. Chile had acquired 18 of these fighters (15 F-5Es and three F-5Fs) but due to the Kennedy Amendment applied in 1974, it lacked spare parts and this reduced their operability. The FACh Tigers had to deal with the Argentine Mirage IIIEAs, and their Hawker Hunters would do the same with the A-4s. But the FACh was going through a critical situation in relation to the spare parts for its combat aircraft, thus not all of them were available to deal with the situation.

Both countries were moving troops in numbers not seen since the War of the Triple Alliance against Paraguay of 1864–1870, and the Chaco War of 1932–1935 between Paraguay and Bolivia. The

Two Hawker Hunter FGA.Mk 71 single-seater and a T.Mk 72 two-seater from Aviation Group No. 8 flying in the Antofagasta area. (FACh)

Hawker Hunter instructors at Los Cerrillos Air Base, 21 March 1974. From left to right: Captains Hernán Gabrielli Rojas (*Geminis*), Egidio Machuca Ramos (*Mohicano*), Raúl Tapia Esdale (*Tauro*), Joaquín Urzua Ricke (*Urano*), Eitel Von Mullembrock Hevia (*Víbora*), Marcos Meirelles Guizman (*Samurai*), Pedro Merino Núñez (*Mercurio*) and Danilo Catalán Farías (*Kangaroo*). (Rino Poletti Collection)

Argentine Navy Light Cruiser ARA *General Belgrano* (C-4 left) and the Aircraft Carrier ARA *25 de Mayo* (V-2 right). (Histarmar Archives)

troops were transported by all possible means, trains, ships, aircraft, and even truck convoys to the south.

Around 12 December, the Argentine fleet, led by the aircraft carrier ARA *Veinticinco de Mayo* and the cruiser ARA *General Belgrano*, arrived in Tierra del Fuego and stationed itself to the east of Isla de los Estados to await instructions. For a few days, its Chilean counterpart had been anchored between the fjords and islets of the

TABLE 1: FACh Operational Deployment on 22 December 1978				
Wing/Location	Aviation Group	Aircraft	Operational	Distribution
1 (Antofagasta)	7	F-5E F-5F	15 2	7 (Antofagasta), 4 (Santiago), 4 (Iquique) 2 (Antofagasta)
	8	Vampire Hunter	6 13	2 (Iquique), 4 (Calama) 13 (Antofagasta)
	9	Hunter	12	6 (Puerto Montt) 6 (Punta Arenas)
	Liaison Squad	C-47 T-41 S-55T	2 1 2	2 (Antofagasta) 1 (Antofagasta) 2 (Antofagasta)
2 (Quintero)	2	HU-16B CSR-110 S-55T	3 2 1	3 (Quintero) 2 (Quintero) 1 (Quintero)
	11	99A	6	3 (Quintero), 2 (Cavancha), 1 (Santiago)
3 (Punta Arenas)	6	DHC-6	5	5 (Margot/ Punta Arenas)
	12	A-37B	7	7 (Chabunco/ Punta Arenas)
4 (Iquique)	1	A-37B	13	13 (Iquique)
	4	A-37B T-25	13 7	8 (Puerto Montt), 5 (Chabunco/ Punta Arenas) 7 (Coyhaique/ Aviation Group 16)
5 (Puerto Montt)	5	DHC-6	9	9 (Puerto Montt)
(Temuco)	3	SA.315B UH-1H UH-12SL4 47D-1	3 8 1 1	6 (Antofagasta and Iquique), 2 (Punta Arenas), 3 (in the Lonquimay sector) 1 (Temuco) 1 (Temuco)
(Santiago)	10	C-47A DC-6B C-130H UH-1H SA.330F	5 5 2 02 01	Los Cerrillos Scattered in several locations Scattered in several locations Los Cerrillos Los Cerrillos
(Santiago)	SAF*	DHC-6 A.100 35A	02 01 02	Los Cerrillos Los Cerrillos Los Cerrillos
(Santiago)	Aviation School	T-34 T-37	24 16	Villarrica and Pucón/Aviation Group 15 7 (Santiago), 9 (Temuco) /Aviation Group 14
*Servicio Aerofotogramétrico (Aerophotogrammetric Service)				

Beagle Channel and the Strait of Magellan, expectantly awaiting the start of hostilities.

For the protection of the Chilean capital, Santiago, the so-called Defence Fighter Squadron No.71 would operate from the Pudahuel International Airport with four F-5E fighters that would be on alert 24 hours a day. Additionally, there were also several armed T-34 Mentor and T-37 Tweety Bird training aircraft, both types capable of carrying out night operations with the assistance of an Airborne Early Warning Beechcraft 99A. In addition, No.1 Anti-aircraft Battery in Pudahuel would protect the F-5Es and also No.2 Anti-aircraft Battery in El Bosque. There would also be a two-dimensional Philips radar in the vicinity of Pudahuel, with an

(Left) Commander Hernán Gabrielli Rojas (*Géminis*) with an F-5E Tiger II of the Aviation Group Number 7, Pudahuel Air Base, November 1978. (Right) Group Captain (A) Mario Villalobos Milic (*Villano*), an F-5 pilot, ready for a sortie in the Santiago area in 1978. (FACh)

effective range between 60 and 120 nautical miles. In addition, there would be a network of ground observers that would operate in the facilities of the Civil Aeronautics Directorate and the Carabineros, also in the hills near the capital, all linked with radio equipment for early warning. The high command of the metropolitan area would be near Pudahuel Airport and would be in charge of the personnel of the FACh Air Warfare Academy under the command of its director, Colonel Fernando Silva Corvalán, for the management of all operational and logistical information, as well as damage control, civil and military air traffic control. By 22 December, the FACh had completed its operational deployment as shown in Table 1.[2]

2

H-HOUR OF D-DAY

In the first days of December, the Argentine Navy Sea Fleet sailed towards the Beagle Channel under the command of Rear Admiral Humberto José Barbuzzi, a veteran sailor who, in 1964 as a corvette captain, had commanded the minesweeper ARA *Seaver*, on board of which he had carried out patrols on the Paraná and Uruguay rivers as well as several exercises in the Río de la Plata. A year before the outbreak of the crisis, Barbuzzi had been appointed Naval Secretary General, a position he held until the Military Junta appointed him Chief of Operations of the General Staff of the Navy to replace Rear Admiral José Néstor Estévez.

At that time, the Argentine naval force was one of the most powerful in Latin America, made up of an aircraft carrier, a cruiser, four destroyers of the First Naval Division, five destroyers, two corvettes, three ocean tugs, three landing ships, six minesweepers, one transport ship, one tanker of the Second Naval Division and also several tankers belonging to the company YPF (*Yacimientos Petrolíferos Fiscales*, Fiscal Oilfields) which provided auxiliary services for the Navy. The submarine force was made up of four submarines.

During its journey to the southern tip of the Continent, the fleet was divided into three battle groups. The First Battle Group was led by the aircraft carrier ARA *Veinticinco de Mayo*, with its Air Naval Carrier Group (*Grupo Aéreo Embarcado*), made up of eight Douglas A-4Q Skyhawk attack aircraft, four Grumman S-2 Trackers, four Sikorsky S-61D4 Sea King helicopters and one Alouette helicopter; the missile destroyer ARA *Hércules* equipped with two Exocet MM-38 missiles, and the then ultramodern A-69-class missile corvettes ARA *Drummond* and ARA *Guerrico* in escort functions, each equipped with another four Exocet MM-38 missiles. The Second Battle Group was headed by the venerable cruiser ARA *General*

(Left and centre) The LST ARA *Cabo San Antonio* (Q-42) and (right) Dock Landing Ship ARA *Cándido de Lasala* (Q-43). (Histarmar Archives)

Fletcher-Class Destroyer ARA *Rosales* (D-22) in a wartime paint scheme in 1978. (Histarmar Archives)

Destroyer ARA *Bouchard* (D-26). (Histarmar Archives)

Belgrano and escorted by the destroyers ARA *Rosales*, ARA *Hipólito Bouchard* and ARA *Piedrabuena*, in addition to the landing ships ARA *Cándido de Lasala* and ARA *Cabo San Antonio*, the tanker ARA *Punta Médanos* and other units of the state oil company YPF. *Rosales* and *Hipólito Bouchard* each provided four Exocet MM-38s. The Third Battle Group sailed with the destroyers ARA *Py* and ARA *Seguí* in the lead, each armed with four Exocet MM-38s, followed by the ARA *Almirante Storni* and the ARA *Domecq García* serving as escorts.

To this, the four units of the Submarine Force Command (*Comando de la Fuerza de Submarinos*, COFS) must be added and the ocean tug ARA *Comandante Irigoyen* together with the patrol boats of the Speed Boat Group that operated from the Naval Base of Ushuaia, ARA *Indómita* (P-86), ARA *Intrépida* (P-85) and the

torpedo boats ARA *Alakush* (P-82) and ARA *Towora* (P-84), a formidable fleet when compared to the one that Chile then had.

The Naval Aviation Command (COAN) also dispatched its veteran Lockheed SP-2H Neptune, North American T-28 Fennec, Aermacchi MB-326GB and several transport units.

For their part, the ground forces had 120 AMX-13 light tanks, 120 upgraded M4 Shermans, 50 to 60 Mowag Grenadiers, 100 M113s, 100–130 M3/M9 half-track vehicles, 20 to 25 AMX VCIs, 24 AMX self-propelled 155mm guns, Schneider 105/155mm hypomobile guns, 101 Oto Melara 105mm guns, Oerlikon L70 20mm model 1935 guns; Bofors L70 40mm model 1938 guns; 105mm recoilless guns; 90mm M67 shoulder-fired recoilless anti-tank launchers, and 35mm Skyguard systems. In addition, the Army had 26 Bell UH-1H helicopters, nine Aerospatiale AS330L Puma and nine Augusta A.109 Hirundos.

Sumner-class Destroyer ARA *Seguí* (D-25) in Ushuaia. (Histarmar Archives)

Two Higgins-class PT Boats, ARA *Alakush* (P-82 left) and ARA *Towora* (P-84 right). (Histarmar Archives)

Some North American T-28P Fennecs from the Argentine Naval Aviation received a tactical camouflage scheme and were deployed to the La Sara area on the Isla Grande of Tierra del Fuego. The T-28s were armed with machine gun pods and rocket launchers. (COAN)

A North American T-28P Fennec on board the aircraft carrier ARA *25 de Mayo*. (COAN)

In compliance with the orders received, the Air Force deployed a good part of its air fleet composed of Douglas A-4B and A-4C Skyhawk attack aircraft, Mirage IIIEA fighters, BAC Canberra Mk.62 bombers and FMA IA.58 Pucará light attack aircraft.

On 11 December, the Argentine Armed Forces Military Committee met to thoroughly analyse the situation and adopt the pertinent measures. The meeting was at the Libertador Building at 9 a.m., with the participation of the members of the Military Junta, except for Brigadier General Orlando Ramón Agosti, who was in Venezuela leading an official mission. The highest-ranking officers of the three arms participated in the conclave, led by the Commander-in-Chief of the Army, Lieutenant General Roberto Eduardo Viola, his Navy counterpart, Admiral Armando Lambruschini, and the Commander of Air Operations, Brigadier Major Miguel A. Ossés on behalf of Brigadier General Agosti. Along with them were the head of the Joint Chiefs of Staff, Brigadier Major Pablo O. Apella, Foreign Minister Carlos Washington Pastor, Secretary General of the Army, General Reynaldo Benito Antonio Bignone, Vice Admiral Eduardo Fracassi of the Navy, and Brigadier Basilio Lami Dozo of the Air Force. The press did not have access to the meeting and all the assistants carefully analysed the instructions given to Brigadier Pastor in relation to the imminent summit with his Chilean counterpart.

In the afternoon, Lieutenant General Viola summoned the Army's High Command to a meeting on the morning of Thursday, the 14th, in which all division generals and the most senior brigadier general would participate. The meeting concerned the Commander-in-Chief's imminent inspection visit to the units in the south and the decisions taken regarding mobilisation.

Meanwhile, in Santiago de Chile, Foreign Minister Cubillos was preparing to leave for Buenos Aires carrying the proposals from his government and a message from Pinochet to Videla whose content was not revealed. When his plane was about to take-off, an anonymous caller warned of the presence of a bomb aboard. The DC-10, belonging to the Brazilian VARIG airlines, was evacuated and subjected to a rigorous inspection, a measure that delayed its departure until 4:30 p.m. After verifying that it was a false alarm, the aircraft took off, landing in Ezeiza two hours later.

War was about to break out when, in the middle of the Beagle Channel, an Argentine torpedo boat almost sank a Chilean barge a day after Buenos Aires decided to close the passage of trucks between Brazil and Chile. While these events were taking place, Chilean troops were preparing their

A Beechcraft Queen Air B-80 of the Argentine Naval Aviation, in tactical camouflage colours, used as a support aircraft for the T-28s. (COAN)

A BAC Canberra bomber displaying its full weaponry potential. The Canberras were deployed to the Comandante Espora Naval Air Base at the end of 1978. (Dirección de Estudios Históricos de la Fuerza Aérea Argentina)

Among the high-ranking officers at the time of the Beagle Crisis were Brigadier Basilio Lami Dozo of the Argentine Air Force and Brigadier Major Reynaldo Bignone of the Army. Lami Dozo would be Commander of the Argentine Air Force in 1981 and throughout the Falklands War, while Bignone would be the last *de facto* President of Argentina between 1982 and 1983. (Public Domain)

defences on Picton, Lennox, and Nueva Islands by digging trenches, laying barbed wire, laying mines on the beaches, and siting heavy artillery pieces.

As of 13 December, Alouette III helicopters of the Argentine Naval Aviation operated from the Frutilla and La Sara Field Aerodromes on the Isla Grande de Tierra del Fuego, as part of the First Helicopter Group. During this deployment, low-level tactical navigation flights, practice attacks on land and naval targets and flight training in adverse weather conditions missions were carried out, as well as patrol and tactical reconnaissance flights. They were equipped with targeting systems and Albatross rocket launchers. In November of that year there were 19 T-28 aircraft available, forming a squadron that was under the command of Frigate Lieutenant Hugo Ortíz and included, as pilots, Frigate Lieutenants Carlos Oliveira, Héctor Césari, Jorge Grosso, Héctor Lescano and Alberto

(Left) A McDonnell Douglas DC-10-30 of the Brazilian airline VARIG. (Right) The Chilean Minister of Foreign Affairs Hernán Cubillos. (VARIG & Public Domain)

Capelli, Corvette Lieutenants Federico Larrinaga, Héctor Padín and Miguel Uberti, and Midshipmen Marcelo Battlori and Diego Goñi. According to the so-called Operation Thunderbolt (*Operativo Tronador*), the T-28s were assigned to provide close air support missions to the Marine Infantry troops, attacks on small vessels in the Bahía Inútil area, and the riskiest ones consisted of attacking the FACh Hawker Hunter jets in the landing phase in Punta Arenas. An important group of T-28s had their base at the Ranch La Sara, where the airstrip conditions were improved, and anti-aircraft shelters and ammunition depots were built. Another group was stationed in Río Grande. The T-28s were armed with machine gun pods, rocket launchers and could eventually carry bombs as well. During

the months of November and December 1978, all the T-28s deployed in Tierra del Fuego practised firing with machine guns and attacking ground targets with rockets and bombs. In addition, these aircraft carried out reconnaissance flights in Chilean airspace, not too far from the border, with the intention of challenging the FACh alert system in the area.

Naval Aviation North American T-28P Fennecs were used as a test platform for the guided anti-ship missiles called MP-1000 Martín Pescador (Kingfisher). These missiles were developed by the Argentine company CITEFA (Institute for Scientific and Technical Research of the Armed Forces) in the 1970s, with the first tests being in 1975. It was first fired by Captain Rodolfo Castro Fox of the Argentine Navy from a T-28P Fennec. About 60 of these missiles were successfully launched between 1975 and 1977 using a guidance system was similar to the American AGM-12 Bullpup missile. During the Beagle Conflict, at least 12 of these missiles were mounted on T-28P Fennec aircraft deployed to the south and they were also fitted to the Aermacchi MB-326 jets and the IA.58 Pucará. They could also be used from hovering helicopters, for which a wire-guided version

(Left) Personnel from the First Helicopter Squadron of the Argentine Naval Aviation posing with an Alouette III at Tierra del Fuego in 1978. (Right) An Alouette III about to take-off from one of the ships of the Sea Fleet during the Beagle Crisis. Note the tactical camouflage applied to these helicopters. (COAN)

(Left) A flight deck catapult of the aircraft carrier ARA *25 de Mayo* giving clearance for take-off to a North American T-28P Fennec armed with machine gun pods. (Right) Three Naval Aviation pilots pose with a T-28P Fennec armed with locally manufactured air-to-surface missiles MP-1000 Martín Pescador. (COAN)

Midshipman Goñi aboard the North American T-28P Fennec serial 0588/3-A-203 (left). The same naval officer and Petty Officer Ruiz posing with the T-28P serial 0628/3-A-208 in Ushuaia in August 1978 (right). (COAN)

(Left) An MP-1000 Martín Pescador missile mounted on a Naval Aviation Aermacchi MB-326. (Upper right) The Martín Pescador was also tested with the IA.58 Pucará of the Argentine Air Force. (Lower right) The CITEFA MP-1000 Martín Pescador air-to-surface missile. (CITEFA & COAN)

was developed. They were not used in the Falklands War and they were withdrawn from use in the 1990s.

On 14 December, while the tension was growing, an event occurred that revived hopes of a possible peaceful solution: Pope John Paul II sent a clear signal to the presidents of Argentina and Chile that he was willing to mediate to avoid the tragedy. The text of the letter was the same for both presidents:

Mr. President,

I want to direct my attention to the imminent meeting between the Foreign Ministers of Argentina and Chile with the lively hope of seeing the controversy that divides your countries and that causes so much anguish in my soul overcome.

Hopefully the colloquium paves the way for a further reflection, which, avoiding steps that could be susceptible to unforeseeable consequences, allows the continuation of a serene and responsible examination of the contrast. Thus, the demands of justice, equity and prudence will be able to prevail, as a secure and stable foundation for the fraternal coexistence of your peoples, responding to their deep aspirations for internal and external peace, on which to build a better future.

Dialogue does not prejudge rights and expands the field of reasonable possibilities, honouring those who have the courage and sanity to continue it tirelessly against all obstacles.

It will be a request blessed by God and supported by the consensus of your peoples and the applause of the international community.

My call inspires the paternal affection that I feel for those two nations so dear to me and the confidence that comes from the sense of responsibility that they have shown up to now and of which I expect a new testimony.

With my best wishes and my Blessing.

Vatican, 12 December 1978

IOANNES PAULUS PP. II[1]

By then, Rear Admiral Barbuzzi had stationed his naval units east of Isla de los Estados, some 300 miles southeast of the Río Grande, deploying nearly all of his ships over the shallow waters of the Burdwood Bank, sheltered from possible action by submarines. Here he was waiting for the order to launch the attack when, around noon on Friday 15 December, he received information that the radar screens had detected an echo. Early in the morning a Chilean Naval Aviation Embraer EMB-111 Bandeirulha had taken off from its base in Punta Arenas towards the Atlantic Ocean. During the flight,

Left to right Lieutenant General Jorge Rafael Videla, *de facto* President of Argentina (1976–1981), His Holiness Pope John Paul II (1978–2005) and Captain General Augusto Pinochet Ugarte, *de facto* President of Chile (1973–1990). (Public Domain)

The Italian Cardinal of the Catholic Church Monsignor Antonio Samoré, appointed by Pope John Paul II as his representative on 24 December 1978 in the mediation of the Beagle Conflict between Argentina and Chile. (Public Domain)

its crew saw a merchant tanker which obviously was part of the FLOMAR (*Flota del Mar*/Sea Fleet) logistic chain. The Bandeirulha landed in Puerto Williams where the crew boarded a Naval Aviation CASA C.212 Aviocar, serial N-146, with a Bendix radar, to continue with the mission, heading east in search of the Argentine Sea Fleet. At 2:40 p.m., at the southeast of Isla de los Estados, flying at 150 knots and 5,000 feet, the Chilean CASA was intercepted by two Argentine Naval A-4Q Skyhawk attack jets, serials 0654/3-A-301 under the command of Corvette Captain Julio Italo Lavezzo and 0660/3-A-307, piloted by Corvette Captain Julio Alberto Poch, that had taken off from the aircraft carrier ARA *Veinticinco de Mayo*. Some minutes earlier, the Skyhawks had begun to be vectored towards

two echoes. The first turned out to be an Argentine Navy Grumman S-2 Tracker flown by Frigate Lieutenant Enrique Fortini and Midshipman Marcelo Álvarez, which was flying with his identification friend or foe system activated, but the second was the Chilean Aviocar, towards which both headed, ready to shoot it down.

When Corvette Captain Lavezzo had the intruder within firing distance, he called his controller for instructions but the Chilean CASA C-212 turned at high speed and, hidden in the clouds, escaped towards Punta Arenas, without accomplishing its mission. Four minutes later, three other A-4Q Skyhawks took off from ARA *Veinticinco de Mayo* with orders to pursue and intercept possible enemy planes, but they did not establish contact.

Throughout that day, the Chilean fleet remained quiet in the fjords, very close to the O'Brien Channel and barely 100 miles from Cape Horn, awaiting instructions. That same night the CIA informed the White House that the Argentine attack was imminent and that it would take place no later than 21 or 22 December, without specifying the exact time. In view of this, the American President Jimmy Carter hastened the return of his Secretary of State, Cyrus Vance, who was on tour abroad at the time.

On 17 December, Admiral López ordered the Chilean Sea Squadron be divided into two groups:

The first group was called *Alpha* or *Steel* and included the warships *Prat*, *Cochrane*, *Blanco*, *Zenteno* and *Portales*. Its mission was to monitor the waters of the Strait of Magellan in case the Argentine Sea Fleet decided to penetrate the area through that zone. Its strength lay in the firepower of its naval artillery.

The second group was called *Bravo* or *Bronze* and included the missile-armed warships *Williams*, *Riveros*, *Lynch* and *Condell*. Later *Latorre* joined this group. All these vessels were capable of firing Exocet anti-ship missiles, in total being able to simultaneously launch 16 missiles against 16 different targets. This group was in the Cape Horn area and its mission was to guard the waters of the Drake Sea, the Nassau Bay area, the Beagle Channel and the areas adjacent to the Horn,

(Left) CASA C.212-100 serial 146 of the Chilean Naval Aviation that was intercepted by two Douglas A-4Q Skyhawks of the Argentine Navy, including serial 3-A-301 (shown right) crewed by Corvette Captain Julio Italo Lavezzo. Both Skyhawks were armed with AIM-9B Sidewinder missiles. (Via Claudio Cáceres Godoy and Juan Carlos Cicalesi)

Barnevelt, Evout, Picton, Nueva and Lennox islands.

These two naval groups were supported by another 18 amphibious and auxiliary ships, in addition to the submarine *Simpson* and the tanker *Araucano*. Additionally, the training ship ACH *Esmeralda* was fitted out as a hospital ship and sailed south under the command of Captain Víctor Larenas.

The Chilean Naval Aviation's Maritime Patrol Squadron with its Embraer EMB-111 Bandeirulhas had been deployed to Punta Arenas, while the Alouette III helicopters were embarked on different ships of the Sea Squadron.

On 19 December in the morning hours, following directives from the High Command, the Argentine Navy Sea Fleet abandoned its positions to the east of the Isla de los Estados and sailed at 20 knots towards the Beagle Channel and Cape Horn in a rough sea, with strong winds blowing from the west and waves that reached four metres in height.

An undetermined number of anti-submarine and anti-surface search missions were carried out by the Argentine Naval Aviation, following from a distance the movements of the Chilean Sea Squadron that operated in the area, for which it was necessary to penetrate Chilean airspace. In one of these actions on 19 December 1978, Lockheed SP-2H Neptune, serial 2-P-111, carried out a clandestine mission of just over eight hours duration. The aircraft took off from Río Grande with a full load of anti-submarine weapons, heading

(Left) The second A-4Q involved in the interception of the Chilean CASA C.212, serial 3-A-307, can be seen here in the middle, on the flight deck of the aircraft carrier ARA *25 de Mayo*. (Right) Corvette Captain Julio Alberto Poch, pilot of 3-A-307. (COAN)

(Left) The two Leander-class frigates of the Chilean Navy together with the oil tanker ACH *Beagle* anchored in a fjord in the southern zone in December 1978. Note the Exocet missile launchers and Alouette III helicopters on both frigates. (Right) A Chilean Navy PT Boat, barely visible, camouflaged with a net in the Austral zone. (Archivo Histórico de la Armada de Chile)

(Left) United States President James 'Jimmy' Earl Carter Jr. (1977–1981).
(Right) Secretary of State Cyrus Vance (right). (Public Domain)

for the Drake Sea Passage, south of the large island of Tierra del Fuego. First the Neptune headed west and then north, flying over the Pacific Ocean at all times to finally return to Argentine airspace through the Strait of Magellan. The information obtained in this mission, together with other data, served to give broad intelligence of the movements of Chilean naval units.

At that same moment, Ambassador Enrique Ros, the Argentine representative to the United Nations, kept in his briefcase the document that he had to present to the Security Council and boarded a vehicle from the legation that was supposed to take him to the organisation's headquarters. It concerned the complaint that his government presented before '...the illegal measures adopted by Chile that, due to their military nature, entailed a renewed danger for international peace and security, since they alter the status quo of the region,'[2] that is to say, the justification for initiating the invasion. The idea was to show the Council that Chile was the aggressor nation

The Chilean Sea Squadron moving to their combat positions in December 1978. (Archivo Histórico de la Armada de Chile)

(Left) The Chilean submarine ACH *Simpson* with the Polar Boat ACH *Piloto Pardo*, with two Naval Aviation Bell 206B/ SH-57A Jet Ranger helicopters on the flight deck. (Right) The tanker ACH *Araucano*, sailing in a choppy ocean and supplying two ships of the Chilean Sea Squadron. (Archivo Histórico de la Armada de Chile)

Two Brooklyn-class light cruisers that would have engaged in combat if a 'shooting war' between Argentina and Chile had broken out: The Argentine Navy's ARA *General Belgrano* (C-4 left) and the Chilean Navy's ACH *Capitán Prat* (right CL-03). (Esteban Raczynski Collection)

and that it was occupying Argentine territory, causing a 'casus belli'[3] that allowed its neighbour to recover 'what belonged to Argentina' through force.

While this was happening in distant New York, the Chilean ships remained in their hiding places when, at 04:49 a.m., one of their planes, the Naval Aviation CASA C-212 Aviocar serial N-147, had two contacts on its radar. On the aircraft carrier ARA *Veinticinco de Mayo*, Frigate Lieutenant Pettinari was waiting on Alert 5 on the deck, aboard A-4Q Skyhawk serial 0654/3-A-301, when he received the order to take-off and intercept the enemy. After checking his

Lockheed SP-2H Neptune, serial 2-P-111 of the Argentine Naval Aviation, carried out a clandestine mission of just over eight hours over Chilean territory on 19 December 1978. (COAN)

Another interception: (Upper) CASA C.212 serial 147 of the Chilean Naval Aviation was intercepted by the Douglas A-4Q Skyhawk serial 3-A-301 of the Argentine Naval Aviation, crewed by Frigate Lieutenant Pettinari. (Lower) The same A-4Q is seen being launched from the catapult of the aircraft carrier ARA *25 de Mayo*. (Via Claudio Cáceres Godoy & COAN)

That same morning, Vice Admiral López Silva, commander of the Chilean fleet operations, was attentively following the news on *Radio Minería* through his battery-operated radio, when he heard the Argentine Foreign Minister say, of Chile, that the time for words had run out and the time for action had begun. Wasting no time, he got up and went to the bridge to order his ships to be ready to sail, following the usual preparations for combat.

It was at that moment that a coded message from the Naval Command arrived at the flagship, alerting the ships to the imminence of the invasion: 'Prepare to initiate war actions at dawn. Imminent attack. Good luck.'[4]

At 10:20 that same day, López Silva received a second message from Admiral Merino that read: 'Attack and destroy any enemy ship in Chilean territorial waters.'[5]

Both Chilean naval groups set sail from their war anchorages on the same day, 19 December, to a point located much further south than Cape Horn, with the intention of preventing any Argentine attempt to land in the disputed area, whether or not it was supported by the Argentine Navy's Sea Fleet, and take advantage of any favourable situation to defeat its naval power. Shortly afterwards, US intelligence sources confirmed to the Chilean government that the attack was going to take place the same night. At 9:50 p.m., the commander of the destroyer ACH *Williams*, Captain Ramón Undurraga, went to the safe aboard his ship to get the key that opened the console controlling the Exocet MM-38 missiles.

At 8 a.m. on Wednesday 20 December, both Chilean naval groups abandoned the positions in the strait and headed south, through the Drake Sea, and began an advance in wedge formation, led by the frigate ACH *Condell*, which had the most modern radar. Around 300 nautical miles to the east, Argentine Navy Admiral Barbuzzi was facing a terrible storm with impressive waves of 12 metres in height and a rough sea that threatened to worsen, a situation that made any approach to the islands unimaginable. And that was what he ordered to be transmitted to the communications room of the

dashboard and verifying that everything was in order, the pilot gave maximum power to his turbines and carefully observing the signalmen's instructions, took off at high speed, heading west.

The Argentine Skyhawk intercepted the Chilean CASA and Pettinari manoeuvred his aircraft alongside the enemy plane, causing it to jerk violently with the force of its turbine, and when he had it marked on his head up display, he asked the tower for permission to shoot it down, but the order never came. The Chilean aircraft fled at full speed, hidden in the clouds, while the Skyhawk turned and headed back to the aircraft carrier.

The Commander-in-Chief of the Chilean Navy Admiral José Merino (centre) and the Commander of the Sea Squadron Vice Admiral Raúl López (first from the left), greeting the Commanders of the Torpedo Boats Corvette Captains Gause and Camacho and the Commander of LCU (Landing Craft Utility) 98, in December 1978. (Archivo Histórico de la Armada de Chile)

Chilean Navy Destroyer ACH *Williams* (DD-19) in the Fuegian channels in the south of Chile. (Esteban Raczynski Collection)

that had been entrusted to him. On the upper deck was the Commander-in-Chief of the Squadron, Vice Admiral Raúl López Silva, who watched another monitor that also gave him vital information: the disposition of the other ships that made up the squadron.

On board the Argentine ships, meanwhile, the personnel knew that in little more than four hours the enemy fleet was going to be detected and for that reason, all measures had been taken to initiate action. However, the storm continued to punish the area and even seemed to get worse.

A new incident then occurred which seemed to indicate that the attacking forces had begun the invasion. As the surface units moved through the rough waters off Cape Horn, one of the ships made sonar contact at position 278, classified as a possible submarine. Once the information was transmitted, instructions were received to attack it immediately and without wasting time, the Argentine Naval Aviation Sikorsky S-61D-4 Sea King helicopter, serial 2-H-231, was dispatched to the objective, which, under a cloudy sky, left the deck of ARA *Veinticinco de Mayo*. The helicopter carried under its fuselage an American-made MK.44 anti-submarine torpedo made up of four sections, the first, located in its blunt nose, carried the 75-pound (34kg) active sonar seeker with the high-explosive warhead immediately behind.

Upon reaching the target, the operator prepared to fire, but when the button was pressed, the projectile did not detach. The helicopter withdrew, but its escort fired several hedgehogs that, although they exploded, did not show any evidence of having made an impact.

Behind the helicopter came a Grumman S-2 Tracker that at 08:45 dropped a torpedo with identical characteristics, which was lost in the depths without reaching the target. Forty minutes later, the Sea King with the faulty torpedo landed on ARA *Veinticinco de Mayo* and with the help of on-board personnel tested its launch system, which then fired perfectly.

It was never known what produced that echo in the sonar, although it is certain that it was not an enemy ship since, at that time, the only submarine that the Chilean squadron had was in Pacific waters, several kilometres away from there.

Libertad Building, the Headquarters of the Naval Command in Buenos Aires, when he realised that the weather was tending to get worse. Faced with this situation, the High Command ordered him to move back pending an improvement in atmospheric conditions, an order that the sea units proceeded to comply with as of 08:15 a.m. on the same day. A Chilean Naval Aviation aircraft informed the naval groups that the Argentine Sea Fleet had changed course, withdrawing from the area.

Absolute silence reigned on the cruiser ACH *Capitán Prat*. On the early morning of 22 December 1978, the flagship of the Squadron advanced in the solitude of the cold southern channels towards the Drake Sea. In command was Captain Eri Solís Oyarzún. In his command post, sitting in front of the monitor, he had minute by minute all the information he needed to know about the other ships of the squadron. The data he received allowed him to have a clear vision of what was happening in order to accurately direct the operations of the ships towards the fulfilment of the mission

Ship Commanders of the Chilean Navy Sea Squadron in 1978. Seated, from left to right, Captains Huber (ACH *Riveros*), Grez (ACH *Araucano*) and Rivera (Navy Chief of Staff) Vice Admiral López (Sea Squadron Commander), Captains Solís (ACH *Prat*), Undurraga (ACH *Williams*) and Conn (ACH *Condell*). Standing, from left to right, Corvette Captain Bolelli (ACH *Aldea*), Captains Sepúlveda (ACH *Portales*), Ramírez (ACH *Lynch*), García (ACH *Zenteno*) and Aguirre (ACH *Cochrane*), and Frigate Captain Fellay (ACH *Blanco Escalada*). (Archivo Histórico de la Armada de Chile)

In the early hours of that same day, at 06:15, the Chilean ambassador to the Vatican, Héctor Riesle, called the Ministry of Foreign Affairs of his country to inform the minister that Cardinal Agostino Casaroli, Secretary of State of the Vatican, had stated that Pope John Paul II was willing to personally intervene to prevent war. The Pontifical official proposed to send a representative to both capitals in order to obtain direct and concrete information on the position of each country, something that he also made known to the Argentine representative in the Vatican. It was also learned that the Apostolic Nuncio in

Sikorsky S.61D-4 Sea King serial 2-H-231 of the Argentine Naval Aviation. (COAN)

Buenos Aires, Monsignor Pío Laghi, had made the corresponding arrangements and that the Cardinal Primate himself, Raúl Primatesta, had sent an urgent cable to Rome, dated 19 December, begging the Holy Father for his immediate intercession. As soon as he finished talking with Riesle, Cubillos ran to La Moneda to communicate the news to President Pinochet who, after listening carefully, ordered him to respond immediately, in the affirmative.

The Argentine response arrived at 1:30 p.m. and fell like a bombshell amongst the government of the neighbouring country; it was a resounding 'no' that perplexed the Chilean officials, who looked at each other, first astonished and then intensely indignant.

At 5:30 p.m. on 20 December, the Argentine ground units took up positions and began preparations to commence the invasion. In the Morro Chico sector, 26 M4 Sherman tanks started their engines and anti-aircraft artillery focused their sights on the targets.

Almost at the same time, A-4Q Skyhawk aircraft took off from ARA *Veinticinco de Mayo* and 20 minutes later they landed at Río Grande Air Base where technical personnel were waiting for them ready to work on their set-up and conditioning. To counteract the attack, the Chileans moved 12 Sherman M4 tanks and numerous 105mm guns towards Cabeza de Mar, while troops aboard trucks hurriedly headed towards Morro Chico.

At 6:15 p.m., shortly after a Chilean naval CASA 212 gave notice of the advance of the Argentine naval units, three FACh Cessna A-37 Dragonfly light attack aircraft under the command of Captain Herrera, took off from Chabunco on a new reconnaissance mission

over the Cabeza de Mar area. The aircraft climbed one after the other until they exceeded the cloud ceiling that covered the area, at an altitude of 700 metres, then headed east, in the direction of the aforementioned point. Near it, their radars picked up an electronic signal that identified their own aircraft, confirming that it was a message sent by Brigadier General Carol Lopicic, commander of the 5th Army Division, from his underground command post located between Kon Aysén and Cabeza de Mar. The encrypted cable ordered a mission over its sector plus instructions with the coordinate code and a list of additional data for the recognition of a border control polygon between Monte Aymond and Río Gallegos Chico. Once the target was confirmed, Captain Herrera, who was carrying the air navigation chart on his right leg, recognised the shooting range and headed towards it, followed

Sherman tanks of the armies of Argentina (left) and Chile (right). (Public Domain)

Part of Aviation Group No.1, based at Iquique in the north of Chile, was deployed to Puerto Montt and Punta Arenas during the Beagle Crisis. (Left) Some of the pilots from that group (with their respective nicknames) in Puerto Montt posing with their Cessna A-37B Dragonfly aircraft. (Right) An A-37B flying over the Beagle area in 1978. (FACh)

On 20 December 1978, Chilean Naval Aviation CASA C.212 serial 145, on a mission in the Beagle area, was intercepted by an Argentine Naval Aviation Douglas A-4Q Skyhawk. (Dirección de Estudios Históricos de la Armada de Chile)

Argentine Naval Aviation Douglas A-4Q Skyhawk serial 3-A-309 piloted by Corvette Lieutenant Marcelo Márquez, who requested authorisation for shooting down the Chilean CASA C.212, which was denied. This officer would die in combat during the Falklands War in 1982 aboard A-4Q serial 3-A-314 when he was attacking the British Royal Navy Frigate HMS *Ardent*. (COAN)

(Left) General Bernardo O'Higgins Military School. (Right) Captain General Augusto Pinochet attending the graduation ceremony at the Military School. (Ejército de Chile)

by his wingmen at a height of 600 metres, flying over the Altos de Terramontes, near San Gregorio.

At 11:30 a.m. a new air incident took place in which an A-4Q Skyhawk crewed by Navy Lieutenant Marcelo Márquez, who would die heroically in combat less than four years later, in the South Atlantic War, intercepted a third Chilean Navy CASA 212 Aviocar, serial N-145, that was flying east in search of the Argentine Sea Fleet. Lieutenant Márquez took aim and immediately afterwards contacted his base requesting permission to shoot him down. The answer was a negative. The Chilean aircraft abandoned the search and quickly fled to San Sebastián, landing half an hour later in Punta Arenas. The Argentine pilot undertook the return and did the same in Río Grande where he proceeded to post the report in the pilots' room, offering a detailed account of his interception.

President Pinochet was presiding over a graduation ceremony for officers at the Libertador Bernardo O'Higgins Military School when his aide-de-camp, Colonel Jorge Ballerino, hurriedly approached him to deliver an urgent message from Punta Arenas. The President read its contents in silence and immediately afterwards put the paper in one of his pockets. The actions had begun.

Pedro Daza, special envoy of the Chilean Foreign Ministry in Washington, was ready to request at the Organization of American States (OAS) the urgent convocation of the TIAR (*Tratado Interamericano de Asistencia Recíproca*, Inter-American Treaty of Reciprocal Assistance) when the CAPE (Strategic Political Advisory Committee) met on the 10th floor of the Diego Portales Building to decide whether to resort to the International Court or not. It was known that, in the event of doing so, Argentina would take the event as 'casus belli' and there would be no turning back, as Argentine Interior Minister Albano Eduardo Harguindeguy had told the Chilean ambassador in Buenos Aires, Sergio Jarpa Reyes. For this reason, after listening to the arguments in silence, Pinochet decided to postpone the initiative for another 24 hours.

3

OPERACIÓN SOBERANÍA

Argentina's *Operación Soberanía* (Operation Sovereignty) had four stages:

Stage 1: Foreign Policy, which included a variety of political-diplomatic actions before the UN (United Nations) and the OAS, to demonstrate Argentina's 'pacifist' position in contrast to Chile's 'warmongering' position.

Stage 2: Territorial deployment of military forces along the border with Chile.

Stage 3: War environment, with night blackout exercises in the main cities, evacuations of the civilian population to air raid shelters, construction of anti-aircraft defences, drills for hospitals, fire-fighters and civil defence. Total closure of the border with Chile. Deployment of combat aircraft to bases near the border with Chile, with aerial bombardment drills, as well as violation of Chilean airspace to measure their reaction capacity and detection systems, as well as the movement of the Sea Fleet (FLOMAR) towards the south.

Stage 4: The attack and invasion of Chilean territory.

As has been previously seen, the Argentine Joint Chiefs of Staff of the Armed Forces prepared an attack plan called *Operación Soberanía* (Operation Sovereignty) in order to recover the disputed islands in the Beagle area. This operation was really a true invasion not only of the disputed islands but of the entire Chilean territory, given the rigidity of the Chilean position on the Beagle problem. The attack would be preceded by a false Argentine complaint to the United Nations Security Council of a military occupation of the islands south of the Beagle Channel by Chile. The Argentine Armed Forces would land on the islands and in the event that the Chilean elite troops that protected the islands offered resistance, the continental territory of Chile would be invaded, searching along the border for the front that offered the least resistance, in order to cut off the country in at least one place and thus force Chile to accept the Argentine conditions.

For this operation, the country was divided into three well-defined zones:

Northwest Theatre of Operations (*Teatro de Operaciones Nor Oeste*, TONO), including the Provinces of Salta, Jujuy, Tucumán, Catamarca, Santiago del Estero, La Rioja, Córdoba, San Juan, San Luis, Mendoza and La Pampa. Its commander was Major General Luciano Benjamín Menéndez.

South Theatre of Operations (*Teatro de Operaciones Sur*, TOS), with the Provinces of Neuquén, Río Negro, Chubut, Santa Cruz and Tierra del Fuego. Its commander was Major General Juan Antonio Vaquero.

Protection Zone (Zona de Protección, ZP), with the Provinces of Formosa, Chaco, Misiones, Corrientes, Entre Ríos, Santa Fe and Buenos Aires. Its Commander was Major General Leopoldo Fortunato Galtieri.

The strategic concept of the plan, in order to achieve the political objective of seizing the islands immediately south of the Beagle that Argentina had proposed, was based on two premises:

That Chile surrendered in a short time as a consequence of the military actions that were being prepared; and

That Chile accept the territorial claims proposed by Argentina, which would be followed by the withdrawal of the Argentine troops from the points of the Chilean territory that had been occupied after the trans-Andean offensive.

As it was expected that the military actions would provoke the immediate reaction of the UN, the United States and other countries, the military planned to carry out a war in the fastest and most violent way, with the aim of seizing the largest amount of Chilean territorial space in a few days, to then accept a ceasefire maintaining a status quo, which would be imposed by the UN, but which would leave Argentina in a position of strength to negotiate the settlement of territories later. To that end, Argentina was more than willing to accept the presence of United Nations peacekeepers to separate the two armies.

From this plan, as of 14 December 1978, the mobilisation stages of the regular forces of the three branches and the partial mobilisation phase of the reservists had been completed. The Argentine offensive on Chile would follow the following sequence:

Phase I
Beginning at 8:00 p.m. (H-2) on D-Day, Friday 22 December 1978, the Argentine Sea Fleet (FLOMAR) and the Marine Corps, Battalion No.5, would occupy Freycinet, Hershell, Wollaston, Deceit and Hornos islands. At 10:00 p.m., (H-Hour), FLOMAR and Marine Battalions No.3 and No.4, would occupy the Picton, Nueva and Lennox islands, also gaining control of the Beagle Channel. The three S61D-4 Sea Kings aboard the aircraft carrier ARA *Veinticinco de Mayo* would transport a section of riflemen from Battalion No.4 of the Marine Infantry to Barnevelt, Evout, Deceit and Hornos islets.

The ground offensive both in Tierra del Fuego and on the mainland would start at midnight (H+2). V Army Corps would attack from the Santa Cruz zone towards Punta Arenas, Puerto Natales and Puerto Eden, trying to conquer the maximum Chilean territory of the Patagonian zone. Simultaneously, the Argentine Air Force would initiate strategic bombing. Once this objective was accomplished, the unit would transfer one third of its forces in support of III Army Corps, which in the central region was to operate over the country's capital and Osorno through the Puyehue Pass and from that point it would continue south in towards Puerto Montt, supported by the advance of the II Armoured Cavalry Brigade.

Subsequently, at 06:00 a.m. (H+8) on 23 December 1978, the Air Force and the Naval Aviation would proceed to destroy the Chilean Air Force on the ground and take Puerto Williams on the Magellan sea coast, with the support of the Sea Fleet, according to what was contemplated within Phase I of the plan.

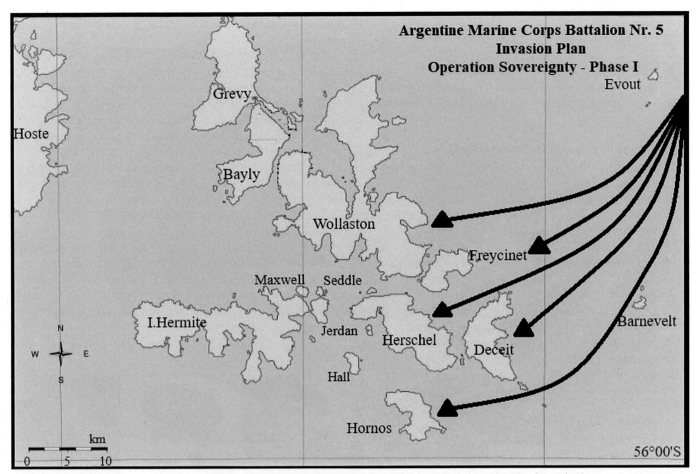

The map shows the beginning of the military operations of *Operación Soberanía*. (Map by author)

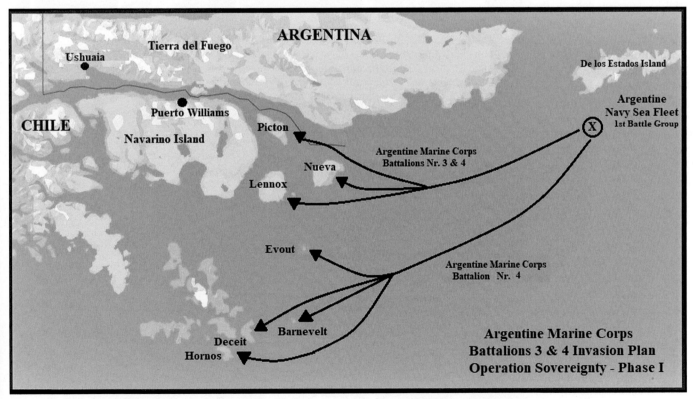

The map shows the occupation of the three disputed islands and some others in the south. (Map by author)

Phase II

This phase provided for the entry of III Army Corps towards Santiago, Valparaíso and Puerto Montt through the Los Libertadores, Maipú and Puyehue mountain corridors, cutting the country in four and conquering as much territory as possible with the support of the Air Force, which would carry out strategic bombardments on enemy positions and specific targets in cities and highways. Based on this plan, the Argentine forces were organised as follows:

Argentine Army

Operation Commander: Lt. General Roberto Eduardo Viola.

II Army Corps: Commander: General Leopoldo Fortunato Galtieri. Assigned mission: Protect the northern border with Brazil and stop any offensive that country could mount against Argentina.

III Army Corps: Commander: General Luciano Benjamín Menéndez.

Assigned mission: Starting from the Mendoza area, cut communications in the centre of Chile, conquering the surroundings of Santiago and, if possible, Valparaíso.

V Army Corps: Commander: General José Antonio Vaquero.

Assigned mission: Strategic offensive starting at midnight (H+2), departing from Santa Cruz, with the probable objective of conquering Puerto Natales and Punta Arenas. Later, it would support III Army Corps in its advance through Puyehue towards Osorno and Puerto Montt, cutting off communications from the central zone to the south of Chilean territory.

In addition, II Armoured Cavalry Brigade would be the reserve, dependent on II Corps, in Comodoro Rivadavia, in charge of preventing a possible Chilean invasion through the Mayo River sector in Chubut.

Argentine Navy

The Navy, with Rear Admiral Humberto José Barbuzzi as the Operation Commander was assigned the mission: to oppose the action of the Chilean Sea Squadron and support the conquest of the islands south of the Beagle Channel. For this, the Argentine fleet had been divided into three task groups (*Grupo de Tarea*/GDT).

The first (GDT 1), was headed by the aircraft carrier ARA *Veinticinco de Mayo*, with its complete *Grupo Aéreo Embarcado* formed by eight Douglas A-4Q Skyhawk attack aircraft, four Grumman S-2 Trackers, four Sikorsky S-61D4 Sea King helicopters and an Aerospatiale Alouette III, with the missile destroyer ARA *Hércules*, with at least two MM38 Exocet missiles, and the brand new Class A-69 missile corvettes ARA *Drummond*,

and ARA *Guerrico*, with four MM38 Exocet missiles each, for escort duties.

The second group (GDT 2) was led by the cruiser ARA *General Belgrano* and the destroyers ARA *Rosales*, ARA *Bouchard* and ARA *Piedra Buena*, the latter two with four MM38 Exocet missiles each; this group would cover the landing force composed of the landing ship (BDD) ARA *Cándido de Lasala* and the tank landing ship (BDT) ARA *Cabo San Antonio*. Also sailing in this task group was the tanker ARA *Punta Médanos* and other tankers from YPF.

The third group (GDT 3), made up of the ARA *Py*, with its four MM38 Exocet missiles, together with the rest of the ships of the First Destroyer Division, the ARA *Seguí*, also with four MM38 Exocet missiles, the ARA *Almirante Storni* and ARA *Almirante Domecq Garcia*.

While the land invasion was taking place, the Navy would launch its different task groups, the first (GT1) in support of the landing on the Channel's islands and the second (GT2) preventing any advance of the enemy squadron towards the Atlantic, while providing support for the troops that would take Gable Island, a step prior to the capture of Puerto Williams.

From left to right, Lieutenant General Roberto Viola (Commander-in-Chief of the Army), Generals Leopoldo Fortunato Galtieri (Commander of II Army Corps), Luciano Benjamín Menéndez (Commander of III Army Corps) and José Antonio Vaquero (Commander of V Army Corps). (Public Domain)

Aircraft of the Carrier Air Group (GAE) of the Argentine Naval Aviation on the aircraft carrier ARA *25 de Mayo*: Sikorsky S.61D-4 (upper left) and Aerospatiale Alouette III helicopters (upper right), Douglas A-4Q Skyhawk attack jets (lower left) and Grumman S-2 Tracker anti-submarine warfare aircraft (lower right). (COAN & Sergio García P.)

Argentine Air Force

Brigadier General Orlando Ramón Agosti would be Operation Commander. The Air Force's objectives were, first, to start bombing military targets in the cities of Punta Arenas and Puerto Williams, and the destruction of the Chilean Air Force, using a technique very similar to that used by Israel in the Six-Day War of 1967. However, in November 1978 FLOMAR had requested strong support from the Argentine Air Force, because one of its fears was the helicopter gunships available to the Chilean Sea Squadron, which could cause a lot of damage.

The Air Force would bombard targets in Punta Arenas, Puerto Williams, Talcahuano, Puerto Montt, and Santiago, seeking as main targets military and political buildings, ports, airports, military bases, bridges, dams, highways, and fuel depots, counting on the fact that, in the first hours of 23 December, its Chilean counterpart would be, if not totally destroyed, reduced by 75 percent. To do this, it had to reach the targets through low-level flight, avoiding detection by radars to attack with its infrared-guided missiles at the moment the Chilean aircraft were about to take-off or were warming up their engines at the head of the runways. The idea was to destroy aircraft and kill pilots so as to completely neutralise the force.

That part of the plan had been called *Operación Muerte Súbita* (Operation Sudden Death) and consisted of hit-and-run attacks on the following targets:

- Quintero Air Base in Valparaíso
- Pudahuel Air Base in Santiago
- El Bosque Air Base in Santiago
- Cerrillos Air Base in Santiago
- Concepción Air Base
- Manquehue Air Base in Temuco
- Pichoy Air Base in Valdivia
- El Tepual Air Base in Puerto Montt
- Balmaceda Air Base in Aysén

This way, all logistical and operational support would be neutralised, leaving the country without air cover and thus obtaining absolute control of the skies.

Aircraft carrier V-2 ARA *25 de Mayo* of the Argentine Navy. Two Alouette IIIs and a Sikorsky S.61D-4 helicopter, and five Douglas A-4Q Skyhawks are visible on the flight deck. (Histarmar Archives)

Two photographs of the light cruiser ARA *General Belgrano* (C-4) in the Beagle area in December 1978. (Histarmar Archives)

Primary targets to be bombed by the Argentine Air Force in Santiago: top row, from left to right, Pudahuel International Airport, El Bosque Air Base and Los Cerrillos Airport. Below, a flight line of Hawker Hunters from Air Group No.7 in Los Cerrillos. (FACh)

Two other FACh air bases to be bombed: El Tepual in Puerto Montt and Quinteros near Valparaíso. (FACh)

Juliet Group: Two BAC Canberra Mk.62 bombers (left) would be escorted by two AMD-BA Mirage IIIEA fighters (right). (Via SOP (Ret) Walter Bentancor & Horacio Gareiso via Vladimiro Cettolo)

According to the plans drawn up by the High Command, the attack would be as follows: The so-called Juliet Group would be launched from El Plumerillo Air Base to attack the Quinteros Base, made up of two Canberra Mk.62 bombers supported by two Mirage III EAs. The Lima Group would be in charge of attacking Pudahuel, El Bosque and Los Cerrillos bases with five A-4B Skyhawks, five A-4C Skyhawks, four Mirages III EAs and three Canberra Mk.62s, also from El Plumerillo Air Base. The Kapa Group would attack Carriel Sur base in Concepción, Manquehue base in Temuco and Pichoy base in Valdivia with three Canberra Mk.62, five A-4Bs, five A-4Cs and four Mirages IIIEAs, from Neuquén Air Base. The Foxtrot Group would do the same to El Tepual Air Base in Puerto Montt, with five A-4Bs, five A-4Cs and four Mirages IIIEAs, presumably from San Carlos de Bariloche. And finally, the Papo Group would raid on Coyhaique with five A-4Bs and five A-4Cs, from Comodoro Rivadavia Base.

Lima & Kapa Groups: Three BAC Canberra Mk.62s (upper left), five Douglas A-4Bs (upper right) and five Douglas A-4Cs (lower left), escorted by four Dassault Mirage IIIEA fighters (lower right). (Dirección de Estudios Históricos de la Fuerza Aérea Argentina)

Foxtrot Group: Five Douglas A-4Bs (left) and Five Douglas A-4Cs (centre) escorted by four AMD-BA Mirage IIIEA fighters (right). (Dirección de Estudios Históricos de la Fuerza Aérea Argentina)

Papo Group: Five Douglas A-4B (top) and five Douglas A-4C (bottom) attack aircraft. On the right, is the very cramped cockpit of an A-4. (Dirección de Estudios Históricos de la Fuerza Aérea Argentina)

The South Defence, in the event of an enemy air attack, would be the responsibility of the Naval Aviation South Group formed by the 11 Douglas A-4Q Skyhawks that operated from the aircraft carrier ARA *Veinticinco de Mayo* and from the Río Grande Air Base, where they also had seven Aermacchi MB-326GBs. There were also some Air Force North American F-86F fighters and Beechcraft T-34A Mentor armed trainers supported by eight A-4Bs and seven A-4Cs from Fighter Group 6 that had been deployed there. The Air Force C-130 Hercules fleet was also essential for transporting troops and heavy equipment.

Some aircraft deployed to the Río Grande Air Base: Douglas A-4Q Skyhawk (upper left) and Aermacchi MB-326GB (upper right) attack aircraft from the Naval Aviation, Argentine Air Force North American F-86F Sabre fighters (lower left) and Beechcraft T-34 Mentors (lower right), the latter armed and camouflaged for close air support. (COAN & Dirección de Estudios Históricos de la Fuerza Aérea Argentina)

All very young and with almost the same uniform, they would have fought each other in case of war and many would not return. Soldiers of the Argentine Army in Chubut in 1978 (left) and soldiers of the Chilean Army (right) in the south of the country that same year. (Public Domain)

The operation estimated that some 200,000 men from both countries would be involved in the war and that Argentine casualties would reach some 5,100 troops, while Chilean casualties would be around 3,200 if a purely defensive deployment was adopted. However, two important newspapers, the Spanish *El País* and the Argentine *La Nación* gave estimates of between 30,000 and 50,000 dead in the course of a total war.

For days D+2 or D+3, the Argentine primary objectives would have been met and an intervention by international organisations was expected for a ceasefire. According to the Argentine theory, it would be time to negotiate a conditional peace with Chile for the cession of territories, especially the islands of the Beagle Channel.

This operation was inspired by both the German Blitzkrieg of the Second World War as well as Israel's Six-Day War against the Arab countries, but there was a big difference. Chile, which was well informed about Argentine military deployments, had prepared to defend its territory. It had placed its troops along the border on

high alert and the Chilean Sea Squadron was already waiting for the Argentine Sea Fleet in the southern sea. There would be no element of surprise. All the student officers of the War and the Polytechnic Academies were assigned to the different theatres of operations, as well as the students of the non-commissioned officers and weapons schools. The Military School only mobilised a company of Ensigns. On the other hand, 100 percent of the reservists with military training had to report to their respective units. The mobilisation order also involved the Carabineros, who had been trained by the Army and incorporated as non-commissioned officers. In total, the Chilean Army mobilised 98,000 effectives.

Besides, what the Argentine High Command could not foresee was that on 21 December the weather worsened with heavy rains, hurricane-force winds and waves of more than 12 metres in height which prevented any approach to the objectives, much less operating with aviation. Even so, Rear Admiral Barbuzzi kept his course towards the area of operations, awaiting the moment

This is a reconstruction of the Aerospatiale SE.316B Alouette II serial number 3-H-111, of the Argentine Naval Aviation. Between 1968 and 2010, Argentinean Naval Aviation acquired a total of 14 Alouette IIIs: they were operated by the 1st Naval Helicopter Squadron, home-based at Naval Air Station Comandante Espora, which maintained regular detachments with the Carrier Air Group embarked aboard the aircraft carrier ARA *25 de Mayo*. In Argentinean service, Alouette IIIs were armed with MG151 20mm calibre automatic guns or 7.62mm MAG machine guns. They could also carry French-made AS.11 or AS.12 anti-tank/anti-ship guided missiles, or A.2445 or Mk.44 anti-submarine torpedoes. (Artwork by Luca Canossa)

Starting in 1971, Argentine Naval Aviation acquired a total of five Sikorsky S.61D-4 Sea King anti-submarine helicopters. They wore serials from 2-H-231 to 2-H-235 and were operated by the 2nd Naval Helicopter Squadron, home-based at Naval Air Station Comandante Espora. The unit regularly deployed detachments of up to four helicopters aboard the aircraft carrier ARA *25 de Mayo*. Fully equipped for anti-submarine warfare, they could be armed with the same torpedoes as the Alouette IIIs, or with depth charges. Like the Alouette IIIs they were at least as often deployed for search and rescue purposes. (Artwork by Tom Cooper)

In 1968, Argentine Naval Aviation purchased eight Aermacchi MB.326GB two-seat jet trainers with combat capability. They received the name *Pelican* in Argentina and were operated by the 1st Naval Attack Squadron, home-based at the Naval Air Station Punta Indio. While primarily serving for jet-conversion and advanced training purposes, they could also be armed with two machine guns of 12.7mm calibre, or up to 1,814kg of bombs and unguided rockets on six underwing pylons. During the stand-off with Chile of 1978–1981, most received a disruptive camouflage pattern, instead of their usual gull grey on top surfaces and sides, and off-white on undersides as illustrated here. (Artwork by Luca Canossa)

Argentine Naval Aviation had been an enthusiastic operator of Grumman S-2 Trackers since the early 1960s, when six S-2As were acquired from the USA. Home-based at Base Aeronaval Punta Indio, later at Base Aeronaval Commandante Espora, they were regularly embarked on the aircraft carrier ARA *Independencia* and then on ARA *Veinticinco de Mayo*. In 1967, six more-powerful S-2Es were acquired: both variants were embarked aboard the ARA *25 de Mayo* during the conflict with Chile in 1978 and flew dozens of maritime and anti-submarine patrols. Indeed, this S-2A – BuAerNo 133257, coded AS-6 (formerly 6-G-53 and 2AS-6) – was the one that tracked the Chilean submarine ACH *Simpson* on 18–19 December 1978. Inset is shown the crest of the sole Anti-Submarine Squadron of the *Comando de la Aviación Naval* of 1978–1981. (Artwork by Tom Cooper)

The principal utility and assault helicopter of the Argentine Army Aviation of the 1970s and 1980s was the Bell UH-1H Huey (shown is the example with the serial number AE-405, applied in black above the fin flash). The first 25 were acquired from the USA in 1969: they entered service with Army Aviation Battalion 601 in early 1970 in their forest green overall livery, as illustrated here, and received serials from AE-400 to AE-424. In October 1978, Buenos Aires acquired six Bell Model 205As from the civilian market: they received serials AE-425 to AE-430. (Artwork by Luca Canossa)

Starting in 1975, the *Fábrica Militar de Aviones* (FMA) in Córdoba manufactured a total of 98 IA.58 Pucará counterinsurgency fighter-bombers. They were distributed between the 3rd Attack Group, III Air Brigade, home-based at BAM Reconquista, and the 4th Attack Squadron, IX Air Brigade, home-based at BAM Comodoro Rivadavia. Pucaras had their cockpits and engines protected from small arms fire by armour, while their internally installed armament consisted of four 7.62mm Browning machine guns. They could carry up to 1,500kg of bombs or unguided rockets on underwing pylons. (Artwork by Luca Canossa)

Starting in 1968, the Argentine Air Force acquired at least 16 Fokker F.27 transports. Eleven were manufactured to the F.27-400M Troopship configuration, and five to the F.27-600 Friendship configuration. They were operated by the 4th Squadron of the 1st Air Transport Group, I Air Brigade, home-based at BAM El Palomar; by the 2nd Air Transport Group, II Air Brigade, home-based at BAM General Urquiza; and by the 9th Air Transport Group, IX Air Brigade, home-based at BAM Comodoro Rivadavia. Time and again, small numbers of Argentine Air Force F.27s were also leased to STAM, LADE (*Líneas Aéreas del Estado*/State Air Lines), and CAME services. (Artwork by Luca Canossa)

Argentine Air Force Boeing 707-387B, serial number TC-91. From 1975 to 2008 a total of seven Boeing 707s saw service in the Air Force: all of them with the 5th Squadron of the 1st Air Transport Group, I Air Brigade, home-based at BAM El Palomar. At the time of the Beagle Crisis, only TC-91 was on strength: this jet wore the usual livery in white on top, a wide cheat line in Argentinean light blue down the fuselage, and light grey along the lower fuselage. The serial number was applied underneath the cargo doors in the forward fuselage, and the service title atop of the upper cabin. (Artwork by Tom Cooper)

The most numerous jet-powered fighter-bomber in service with the Argentine Air Force of the late 1970s and early 1980s was the Douglas A-4B Skyhawk. Fifty were acquired starting in 1966, and they were all operated by the 5th Fighter-Bomber Group, V Air Brigade, home-based at BAM Villa Reynolds. All were painted in dark brown and dark olive green on upper surfaces and sides, and light grey on undersides, and wore three-digit serial numbers in black, prefixed by 'C', applied below the cockpit. Also widespread was the application of the V Air Brigade's crest. Argentinean A-4Bs were typically armed with two internally installed Colt Mk. 12 20mm calibre auto-cannons, but their principal armament consisted of up to five 250kg free-fall bombs, or a single 500kg bomb under the centreline. (Artwork by Luca Canossa)

Another Skyhawk version operated by the Argentine Air Force was the A-4C, a total of 25 of which were purchased beginning in 1975. They were operated by the 4th Fighter Group, IV Air Brigade, home-based at BAM El Plumerillo, and by the 5th Fighter Group, V Air Brigade, from BAM Coronel Pringles. Their primary armament was the same as that of A-4Bs, but they could also be equipped with Israeli-made Shafrir Mk. II infrared-homing air-to-air missiles. That said, the principal difference from the A-4B was their camouflage pattern in light grey and dark olive green, which was better suited for operations in the cold and snowy terrain surrounding the Beagle Channel. Serial numbers on A-4Cs of the IV Air Brigade were usually applied on the rear fuselage or, alternatively, only the 'last two', at the bottom of the rear edge of the fin. (Artwork by Luca Canossa)

One result of the Beagle Channel Crisis was the Argentinean decision in 1978 to purchase 26 refurbished Dassault Mirage 5s from Israel (followed by 13 additional examples, together with 50 Shafrir Mk II air-to-air missiles). These were originally designated *Nesher* in Israel in an effort to cover up a clandestine acquisition of such aircraft from France in the early 1970s. In Argentine service, the type received the name *Dagger*: it entered service with the newly-established Air Group IV, worked up with support of personnel from VIII Air Brigade and the Peruvian air force. Like the Mirage IIIEAs, Argentinean Mirage 5s received the South-East Asia camouflage pattern developed in the USA, and including tan (FS30219), green (FS34102), and dark green (FS34079) on upper surfaces and sides, and light grey (FS36622) on under surfaces. They were usually armed with 250kg bombs and Shafrir air-to-air missiles. (Artwork by Tom Cooper)

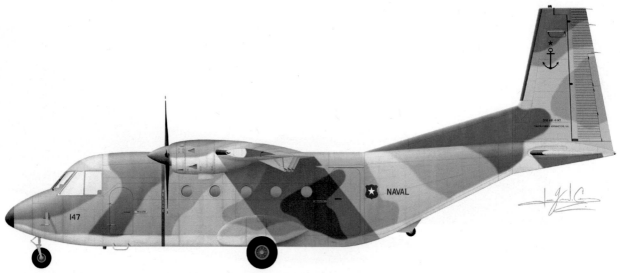

In attempt to bolster its maritime patrol capabilities, in 1978 the Chilean Navy purchased four CASA C.212-100 Aviocar aircraft from Spain. All were in service by the end of the year, being deployed by General Purpose Squadron 1 (VC-1) of the Chilean Naval Aviation – for reconnaissance, and in cooperation with the Naval Aviation Exploration Squadron 1 (VP-1), and for troop and cargo transport. The type proved highly popular in service because of its high reliability, and short take-off and landing capability, and remained in service until 2012. (Artwork by Luca Canossa)

Starting in 1975, the FACh acquired a total of 32 Cessna A-37B Dragonfly light strikers from the USA. They were operated by *Grupo 1*, home-based in Los Cóndores; *Grupo 4*, home-based in Alto Hospicio, outside Iquique; and *Grupo 12*, home-based in Chabunco, in Punta Arenas. The entire fleet wore the same camouflage pattern in tan, earth brown and dark green on top surfaces and sides, and light grey on undersides. They had the GAU-2B/A 7.62mm calibre minigun installed in the nose, and four underwing hardpoints: the inner four were rated for 390kg, and usually used for carriage of drop tanks; the intermediate ones were rated for 270kg, and the outboard pylons for 230kg. Typical armament consisted of Mk.81 and Mk.82 bombs, or LAU-3/A rocket pods. (Artwork by Luca Canossa)

Chile acquired a total of 20 Hunter F.Mk 71s, five FR.Mk 71As, and four T.Mk 72s. In reaction to tensions with Argentina, the technical services of the FACh rushed to overhaul and upgrade several of them. By December 1978, the examples with serial numbers J-702, J-704 (main artwork), J-708 (inset), J-709, and J-724 of *Grupo 9*, reappeared repainted in sand (FS33434), and brown (FS30140), applied to a standardised camouflage pattern on upper surfaces, and sky blue (FS35466) on the undersurfaces. J-702, J-704, and J-708 had no unit insignia, and the first two had their white star applied directly on the rudder painted in mid-stone, without any dark blue colour. While home-based at Cerro Moreno, during the crisis of 1978–1981, most were forward-deployed to Carlos Ibánez airport in the south. (Artwork by Tom Cooper)

Between 1981 and 1983, additional Hunter F.Mk 71s and several FR.Mk 71As of *Grupo 8* had been subjected to overhauls and upgrades. Amongst these were F.Mk 71s with serial numbers J-703 (inset), J-709 and J-710 (main artwork, as seen at Cerro Moreno in 1981), all of which were painted in satin compass ghost grey (FS36320), with a camouflage pattern in ghost grey (FS36375) on upper surfaces and sides. Both J-709 and J-710 further received camera systems from old RT-33s installed in the trolley for the gun pack instead of four ADEN cannons: nick-named '*Hunter ojo*' ('Hunter Eye'), they did not have Sabrina under-fuselage containers. Notably, while fighters frequently carried 100-gallon drop tanks, both of the reconnaissance birds needed 'jumbo' drop tanks for their reconnaissance missions, many of which were clandestine by nature, giving them a more streamlined appearance. (Artworks by Tom Cooper)

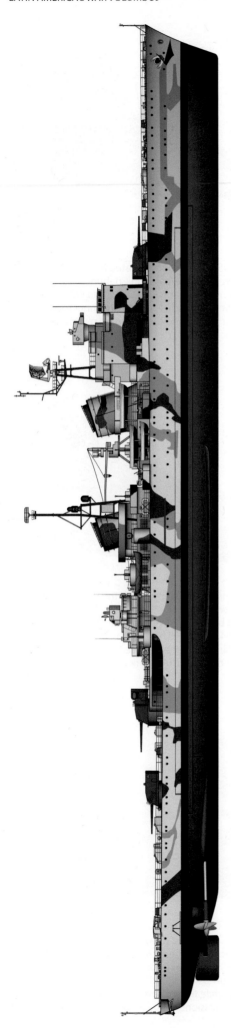

This is a reconstruction of the Tre-Konor-class light cruiser ACH *Almirante Latorre* of the Chilean Navy from the 1978–1981 period. Originally constructed as *Göta Lejon* for the Swedish Navy during the late Second World War, it was acquired by Chile in 1971. The ship displaced 8,332 tons at full load, could reach a speed of 33 knots (61km/h), and had a crew of 445. Principal armament included seven 152mm guns, four 57mm guns, and eleven 40mm guns, all manufactured by Bofors. Delays in the start and construction resulted in this ship being completed only after the end of the War: *Göta Lejon* underwent a refit in the early 1950s, receiving a new bridge and radar. Another refit in 1957–1958 resulted in the installation of the US-made SPS-10 radar atop of the forward mast and revision of secondary armament to the four 57mm guns and eleven 40mm guns. Finally, in Chilean service, the ship received a helicopter deck at the stern. She remained in service until 1984, when she was sold for scrap. (Artwork by Ivan Zajac)

The Allen M. Sumner-class of 58 destroyers was constructed during the Second World War and was perhaps the most successful of contemporary designs and subsequently served as the basis for the Gearing-class. Its primary armament was three twin 5-in/127mm dual gun mounts, and heavy anti-aircraft weaponry. Thanks to FRAM upgrades, most of the ships served in the US Navy into the early 1970s, when they were decommissioned for lack of stand-off anti-submarine warfare capability. Two were then acquired by Chile: the first of these was USS *Douglas H. Fox* (DD-779), transferred in January 1974, when the ship was renamed ACH *Ministro Portales* (DD-17), which is depicted here. This destroyer displaced 3,218 tons when full, could reach the speed of 34 knots (63km/h), and had a crew of 336. Armament included six 127mm calibre dual purpose guns, two triple Mark 32 torpedo tubes for Mark 22 torpedoes, and two racks for depth bombs. The helicopter deck and hangar were suitable for smaller helicopters only. (Artwork by Ivan Zajac)

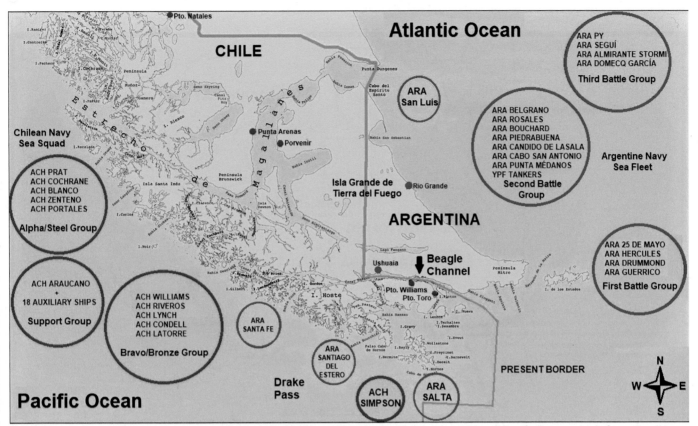

Deployment of Argentine and Chilean naval forces in December 1978 in the South Atlantic and South Pacific Oceans, ready for action (Map by author)

Argentine Reconnaissance Flights

19.12.78: Naval Aviation Lockheed SP-2H Neptune route
22.12.78: Air Force Douglas A-4C Skyhawk route

Between 19 and 22 December 1978, both the Argentine Air Force and the Naval Aviation deliberately violated Chilean airspace to measure the detection and interception capacity of the Chilean Air Force (Map by author)

The Argentine armed forces' plan to invade Chile in December 1978, which was called Operation Sovereignty. The planned counterattacks of the Chilean Armed Forces are also shown. (Map by author)

(Left) Anti-tank defence lines of the Northern Theatre of Operations (Teatro de Operaciones Norte, TON) built with tetrapods. (Right) Large minefields were prepared in the north on the borders with Peru and Bolivia. After the conflict, warning signs were placed in order to avoid accidents. (Public Domain)

The new borders between Chile, Peru and Bolivia, after the War of the Pacific (1879–1884). (Map by author)

when the storm subsided thus initiating the actions.

Chile had also mined large areas of its border with Peru, Bolivia and Argentina in the 1970s and some mountain passes were also closed. The possible use of the northern armies to invade northern Argentine territory in what has been called the left hook strategy, was based on non-participation of Bolivia or Peru in the war. Although it was not decisive, it would occupy extensive, mostly uninhabited territories that, in the media and politically, would have made Argentine advances at any point of Chile look insignificant and could be maintained for future negotiations. Although that would have meant perhaps an unexpected expansion of the conflict, it could have been beneficial for Chile.

It must be remembered that after the War of the Pacific (1879–1884), Chile annexed the Bolivian region of Antofagasta, and the Peruvian regions of Tacna, Tarapacá and Arica, although later, through the 1929 Treaty, Tacna was returned to Peru. Since then, certain Peruvian and Bolivian political and military sectors had been waiting for the opportunity for revenge to try to recover the lost territories.

In 1978, the Chilean strategic defensive plans were called *Hipótesis Vecinal/HV* (Neighbourhood Hypothesis). In that year, Chile was in acceptable conditions to face an HV2 against Peru and Bolivia, but decidedly not a HV1 with Argentina, let alone a HV3 against its three neighbours. A combined army of Peru, Bolivia, and Argentina could rapidly mobilise 234,550 professional soldiers, 650 tanks, 12 submarines, and 389 combat aircraft against only the 85,000 professional soldiers, 146 tanks, 3 submarines, and 97 combat aircraft of Chile.

In the case of Peru, the not-so-distant precedent, back in 1973–1974, was the intention of that country to start a war to reconquer the territories lost in the War of the Pacific of 1879–1884. Beginning in the 1960s, but especially in the 1970s, the Peruvian government carried out an ambitious programme for the purchase or renewal of war material. As the US government had refused to provide Northrop

Presidents of Bolivia in the 1970s: From left to right, Army General Hugo Banzer Suárez (1971–1978), Air Force General Juan Pereda Asbun (July–November 1978) and Army General David Padilla (1978–1979). (Public Domain)

Presidents Pinochet and Banzer met in the Bolivian border town of Charaña in August 1975. Chile offered Bolivia a sovereign strip of land with access to the sea north of Arica, but Peru tenaciously opposed this agreement because it was a territory that had been taken from it in the War of the Pacific. (Public Domain)

The Presidents of Peru between 1968 and 1980: (left) General Juan Francisco Velazco Alvarado (1968–1975) and (right) General Francisco Remigio Moralez Bermúdez (1975–1980). (Public Domain)

F-5E/F Tiger II fighters to the Peruvian Air Force, the government sought combat planes from France and also from the Soviet Union. The Peruvian Armed Forces had acquired from the Soviet Union 450 T-55 tanks, 122mm artillery pieces, SA-2 and SA-3 surface to air missiles and thousands of AK-47 assault rifles for the army and 32 Sukhoi Su-22M-2K Fitter-F and four Su-22M-2D Fitter-E fighters for the air force, as well as 14F and P-37 surveillance radars, P-15 and PRV-11N radars for acquisition and fire control associated with mobile and static batteries of SA-3 anti-aircraft missiles, SA-7 portable missiles and anti-aircraft artillery units of 23mm and

37mm. Additionally, they had also received 25 Dassault Mirage 5P/DP interceptor fighters from France between 1969 and 1976. The Peruvian Air Force also had 28 BAC Canberra B.Mk.8/56/68/72/T.Mk.74 bombers and 36 Cessna A-37B Dragonfly light attack jets on strength. For the Peruvian Navy, the government had contracted for the construction of four missile frigates of the *Lupo* type. After the coup of 11 September 1973, there was a large Peruvian military deployment on the border with Chile, which alarmed the latter government, but with the fall of General Juan Velazco Alvarado's regime in August 1975, and its replacement by that of General Francisco Moralez Bermúdez, relations improved.

The Bolivian army and air force did not constitute a threat to Chile by themselves. The Bolivian Air Force (*Fuerza Aérea Boliviana*, FAB) did not have good infrastructure or proper air bases in the border areas. Its main combat aircraft were obsolete and consisted of seven old North American F-51D Cavalier/Mustang fighters, 10 North American F-86F Sabre fighters, and 10 Lockheed/Canadair CT-33AN Silver Stars ground attack/advanced trainers. Presidents Pinochet and Banzer had met in the Bolivian border town of Charaña in August 1975 to smooth things over. Chile offered Bolivia a sovereign strip of land with access to the sea north of Arica, but Bolivia had to cede a territory of equal size. Peru tenaciously opposed this agreement because it was a territory that had been taken from it in the War of the Pacific. Due to all this, diplomatic relations between Chile and Bolivia deteriorated and ended up with a rupture on 17 March 1978. This rupture with Bolivia, the always cold relations with Peru and the possibility of an alliance between these two countries with Argentina made the Chilean government consider the possibility of a scenario for simultaneous war against the three neighbouring countries.

In the case of the Chilean Army, the Andes mountain range was the main barrier to an invasion, since any incursion by significant forces would have to move through mountain passes, all conveniently mined and defended on the Chilean side. This made any penetration highly risky since the passes

On 21 December 1978, a huge storm occurred in the area of operations of the Beagle, forcing the Argentine Navy and Air Force to postpone the invasion of Chilean territory in the south. The photo on the left was taken from a logistics ship of the Argentine Navy and on the right, the frigate ACH *Condell* of the Chilean Navy, sailing in a very choppy sea. (Histarmar Archives)

(Left) General Guillermo Toro Dávila, Commander of the VI Division of the Chilean Army with President General Augusto Pinochet. (Right) Troops of the VI Division of the Chilean Army wearing a light tan uniform, suitable enough to match the northern environment. (Public Domain)

(Left) Pilots and crew members of the BAC Canberra bombers of the Argentine Air Force. (Centre) A Mirage III fighter pilot, the then 1st Lieutenant Gustavo Argentino García Cuerva. (Right) Lieutenant Carlos Sellés, A-4B fighter pilot. (Dirección de Estudios Históricos de la Fuerza Aérea Argentina)

Crews of the Lockheed C-130E/H Hercules fleet posing with the TC-67 of I Air Brigade of the Argentine Air Force. (Dirección de Estudios Históricos de la Fuerza Aérea Argentina)

(Left) The then Lieutenant Gabriel Pavlovcic (centre) with Non-Commissioned Officers (NCOs) Tillería and Bazán, posing with the Hughes 369 serial H-23 at the Río Mayo Air Base in December 1978. (Comodoro (Ret) Gabriel Pavlovcic).
(Right) Sikorsky S-58T serial H-02 at the Río Mayo Air Base in December 1978. From left to right, Lieutenants Fernández and Arenas, and NCO Cruz. (M. A. Fernández)

could be dynamited at any time, and any advance force that managed to cross could be cut off and destroyed. In the event of a larger invasion, with a significant contingent of Argentine troops in Chile, the Chilean troops would not have sufficient depth of territory to carry out manoeuvres. At some points it would have been relatively easy for Argentinean forces to reach the Pacific and cut Chile into two or more isolated territories. Under these conditions, the Chilean Army would probably have adopted guerrilla tactics against an occupying force, following the tradition of the liberators of mixing amongst the civilians, that of the Mapuche aborigines who avoided the Spanish until they were sure of being able to attack them from an advantageous position. It should be remembered that the National Intelligence Directorate (*Dirección de Inteligencia Nacional*, DINA) managed to carry out attacks in other countries, so it was to be expected that during any eventual urban occupation, the Argentines would have had to deal with a well-prepared enemy.

In addition to the defensive strategy planned by the Chilean Army, it also planned to carry out a counteroffensive on two fronts, so that Chile could sit down to negotiate with Argentina on equal terms. This plan was divided into two stages using boxing terms:

The first stage was a 'left jab' in the north,[1] which would consist of crossing the border and invading the provinces of Salta and Jujuy, taking the main cities, and a 'right uppercut' in the south,[2] that would take place on the island of Tierra del Fuego, with the invasion of the Argentine zone, and the capture of cities such as Río Grande and Ushuaia. This strategy would be put into effect on D+3, the third day of hostilities.

In the naval scenario, the Chilean Navy was comparatively inferior to the Argentine Sea Fleet although it was still a serious threat. In addition, Argentina did not have nautical charts of the fjords and islands of the Pacific, which were used extensively by the Chilean squadron to hide their ships and plan their movements, while the FLOMAR could only travel through the open sea and on known routes generally with heavy seas, such as the Strait of Magellan or Cape Horn. Any alternative route meant a risk of running aground or being exposed to ambush. This, according to the Argentine perspective, was not of importance since it had about 100 aircraft of all kinds flying, to aid in observation, navigation and detection. The Chilean Air Force was significantly inferior to Argentina in technology and numbers. In addition, and given the shape of the

(Left) Maintenance NCOs of the Argentine Army posing with a Bell UH-1H. (Right) Argentine Army Gunners of the UH-1s. (Ejército Argentino)

FACh fighter pilots of the Northrop F-5E/F of the Aviation Group No.7 during the Beagle Conflict in 1978. (Via Sergio Molina)

territory, the country had a very limited capacity for early warning and anti-aircraft defence, all of which allowed Argentina to achieve air superiority.

On 15 December, in view of the worsening of relations between Chile and Argentina, the Peruvian government ordered the departure of the Navy's war fleet to the border with Chile, in addition to putting the Army and the Air Force on alert. Even the Jorge Chávez International Airport in Lima was closed to facilitate Air Force manoeuvres. In addition, in the city of Santa Cruz, Bolivia, high-ranking Peruvian and Bolivian officials met.

Given that the vast majority of air, land and naval military resources were deployed to the south, the Northern Theatre of Operations had to deal with what little remained in the area, under the organisation of General Guillermo Toro Dávila, Commander of the VI Army Division. His command post was installed in an abandoned mine.

On 21 December, at 10:00 p.m., Foreign Minister Hernán Cubillos was meeting with his closest advisers when he was notified that he had an urgent call. Upon answering the phone, he listened carefully to what was being said and after hanging up, informed his team of advisers that the invasion had begun. He was informed that Chilean

FACh Fighter pilots posing with a pair of Hawker Hunters in Puerto Montt, December 1978. (FACh)

FACh Mechanic NCOs, posing with a Hawker Hunter of the Aviation Group No.9. The sign reads 'Danger, Black Panthers Zone.' (FACh)

Cessna A-37B Dragonfly Pilots of the FACh Aviation Group No.12, during the Beagle Crisis of 1978. Standing, from left to right: Lieutenant John Teare Copman, Captain Oscar Fehlandt Schleef, Group Commander Antonio Quirós Reyes, Lieutenant Iván Galán Martínez, Squadron Commander León Duffey Treskow, Lieutenants Renato Valenzuela Taylor and Gabriel Allende Calderón. Seated, from left to right, Lieutenants Mario López Blanc, Tomislav Spasojevic Kistec, Oscar Saa Herrera, Raúl Carrere Iroume and Renato Barría Muñoz. (FACh)

Pilots of the De Havilland DH-115 Vampire of the Aviation Group No.8. (FACh)

Group Commander Sergio Contardo Flores aka Corvo (centre, in flight gear), Commander of Aviation Group No.4, together with his officers and staff of the Group, which operated the Vampire T.Mk.11 and T.Mk.22 fighters, from December 1974 until mid–1976. Subsequently, the last Vampires would serve in Aviation Group No.8 in 1978. (General Sergio Contardo F. Collection)

Chilean Air Force Grumman HU-16B Albatross crews. (FACh)

Pilots and mechanics of the Bell 206B/SH-57A Sea Ranger helicopters of the Chilean Naval Aviation. (Archivo Histórico de la Armada de Chile)

Navy airplanes had detected the Argentine War Fleet in the area of Cape Horn, sailing in attack configuration. The Chilean Navy Fleet was in permanent observation, had taken up defensive positions in the area and the order for action would be issued in minutes. In the Beagle Channel, Vice Admiral López Silva received the order from the Navy Commander-in-Chief Admiral Toribio Merino to set sail immediately and engage the Argentines.

That was the climate that prevailed on both sides of the Andes mountain range when the Pinochet government invoked the TIAR and requested an urgent Hemispheric Consultation meeting to denounce Argentina as an aggressor country while a diplomatic solution was sought that avoided war.

The invasion should have started at 10:00 p.m. on 21 December, but due to a huge storm in the area, it had to be postponed. The helicopters were waiting on deck for the order to leave, but the storm did not abate and the rough sea shook the ships with increasing violence, preventing the start of the operation. Aboard the aircraft, commandos and elite troops waited in silence, holding their weapons tightly in their

Young FACh pilots posing with camouflaged Beechcraft T-34B Mentor primary trainers/light attack aircraft. (FACh)

gloved hands, their faces covered with shoe polish and their heads covered in black wool caps. Pilots and crew members remained on alert, ready to take-off, and on the mainland, thousands of soldiers were preparing to begin the advance. Morale was high with a great desire to fight, but the hours passed and nothing seemed to indicate that the weather would improve.

At 7:19 p.m. another Chilean Navy CASA C.212 was able to confirm the position of the Argentine fleet at 134°, 120 kilometres southeast of Cape Horn, in the midst of a strong storm, but what their radar detected were US ships sailing near that point. In the afternoon, Naval Command had ordered Captain Pablo Wunderlich to move his cadres to Nueva Island because that was going to be the enemy's first target. The officer had embarked the 150 elite troops of his Marine Infantry detachment and aboard the destroyer ACH *Serrano*; he had headed to that destination, taking positions in sight of the enemy.

That same night, at 11:00 p.m., another reconnaissance plane reported that it had detected the fleet moving in the vicinity of the

Channel's islands and that one of the ships was already landing troops. This caused some nervousness to spread among the Chilean forces stationed in the region, but it was immediately learned that the crew of the aircraft had confused the objective because what appeared on their screens at that time were actually the Chilean PT Boats ACH *Quidora*, ACH *Fresia*, ACH *Tegualda* and ACH *Guacolda* which were moving through that sector. Vice Admiral López Silva's sea units were quickly informed of the error and this prevented them from being attacked by their own forces.

Finally, the Argentine High Command gave the order to start the attack and shortly after receiving it, Rear Admiral Barbuzzi issued the corresponding directives, which was done in a massive storm and in the middle of the raging waters of Cape Horn.

On the night of 21–22 December 1978, after 20 days on the high seas and at least one postponement of the start of hostilities, the Argentine ships packed with troops and landing gear continued their advance towards the conflict zone to launch the largest amphibious operation in Latin American history. The invasion had begun.

4

DEPLOYMENTS UNDER THE SEA

Chilean Navy Captain Rubén Scheihing, commander of the submarine ACH *Simpson* (SS-21), knew perfectly well that a comparison between his boat and those of the Argentines would be distinctly not favourable. The Balao-class submarines had been used successfully in the Second World War because they had a

pressurised steel hull that increased their operating depth to 400 feet (122 metres), a detail that differentiated them from the Gato-class, whose structure was reinforced by rings of steel welded together to form a cylindrical tube covered by a second outer superstructure, made them more vulnerable and less efficient. But by 1978, this

The Chilean Navy submarine ACH *Simpson* (SS-21), in the waters of the Pacific Ocean. (Archivo Histórico de la Armada de Chile)

Types of torpedoes used by Chilean and Argentine submarines during the Beagle Crisis in 1978. From top to bottom, a Mk.14, a Mk.27, both used by Chile, and an Argentine Mk.37. (Public Domain)

type of submarine was obsolete, since it lacked a snorkel – a device that allowed the recharging of electric batteries while submerged, feeding diesel engines with air and expelling carbon monoxide. If they had to evade an attack, their batteries would run out quickly, and their ancient Mk.14 and Mk.27 torpedoes were not guaranteed successful, particularly in comparison with the Argentine Navy's modern Mk.37 examples.

Unlike the Guppy-class veterans of the Argentine Navy, which had been upgraded and modernised with state-of-the-art equipment, the *Simpson* did not have a snorkel system. For this reason, the Chilean submarine needed to surface for periods of up to eight hours to recharge its batteries, a situation in which it was extremely exposed to enemy radar. To make matters worse, as has already been stated, its twin, the *Thompson*, had been under repairs because of its very poor condition and served only as a source of spare parts for the *Simpson* during the Beagle Crisis. On the other hand, the modern boats *Hyatt* and *O'Brien* had to return to their bases due to serious damage to their on-board systems. Thus, Chile was at a clear disadvantage regarding the war under the water.

At the time of sailing, Captain Scheihing knew that the four Argentine submarines were operational and that this was going to weigh heavily on the development of the actions. For this reason, he ordered his radio operators to maintain strict control of the communications traffic between the Navy and the Squadron, and to inform them instantly of any news. He was sleeping in his cabin when, at 02:00 on the morning of 21 December, he was awakened by the sound of the receiver. At the other end of the tube, the duty officer informed him that a directive from the Naval Command had just arrived.

(Left) The Chilean Navy destroyer ACH *Blanco Escalada* with the submarine ACH *O'Brien* (S-22).
(Right) ACH *Hyatt* (SS-23) leaving port. (Archivo Histórico de la Armada de Chile)

The Chilean Navy submarine ACH *Thomson* (SS-20), which was under repairs in 1978 and was not
deployed to the south during the Beagle Conflict. (Archivo Histórico de la Armada de Chile)

The Argentine Navy Submarine ARA *Santa Fé* (S-21) at its base in Mar del Plata (left)
and sailing on the surface at sea (right). (Histarmar Archives)

(Left) The Commander of the submarine ARA *Santa Fé*, Frigate Captain Alberto Ricardo Manfrino observing through the periscope. (Centre) A crew member of the ARA *Santa Fe* operating the immersion levers. (Right) Another crew member takes advantage of navigation on the surface of the sea in the Beagle Channel to smoke a cigarette. (Histarmar Archives)

(Left) The submarine ARA *Santiago del Estero* (S-22)of the Argentine Navy at its base in Mar del Plata. (Right) *Santiago del Estero* being assisted by the logistics ship *Aracena* in the southern area during the Beagle Conflict. (Histarmar Archives)

(Left) The submarine ARA *San Luis* (S-32) of the Argentine Navy leaving its base in Mar del Plata. (Right) *San Luis* surfacing in Atlantic waters. (Histarmar Archives)

The Captain went to the command room and read the Admiral's message that ordered him to prevent any Argentine attempt to land on Chilean soil. Immediately after, he read this message to all the crew members on board. Then announced to his men: '…This means that we are in a situation of war with Argentina! As we all know, it is possible that they will sink us, but I promise you that before that happens, at least, we will take two of them!'[1]

The instructions received were precise: any Argentine landing attempt on the Channel's islands was to be prevented, but under no circumstances were they to fire first; the Chileans should only do so in the event of being attacked. It was imperative to make it clear that Argentina was the aggressor country because if Chile initiated hostilities, it would make it impossible to go from victimisers to victims – and that could not be allowed to happen for any reason.

On the Argentine side, things were quite different, since its submarine force had two modern German IKL.209-1200 units, assembled and welded at the Tandanor Shipyards in Buenos Aires, and the old Guppies had been reconditioned, which made them a lethal weapon that would have had the opposing squadron in permanent check. At that time, the Commander of the Submarine Force of the Argentine Navy was Captain Raúl Marino. The submarines began to get ready in mid-November and at the beginning of December they left for the south, the same day that the bulk of the fleet left from Puerto Belgrano. The commanders of the four Argentine submarines deployed in the Beagle area were also ordered not to attack first and to do so only if they were attacked.

Each commander of the submarines received deployment orders as follows: Frigate Captain Alberto Ricardo Manfrino, commander of ARA *Santa Fe* (S-21) received orders to patrol Cook Bay, in the Pacific Ocean, positioning itself halfway between the Hoste, Gordon and Londonderry Islands, the natural access to the Beagle Channel from the west and a necessary passage for the enemy fleet towards Cape Horn. Frigate Captain Carlos M. Sala, commander of the ARA *Santiago del Estero* (S-22), was ordered to position himself further to the southeast, in the vicinity of Caroline Island, a place of rough waters that would put his crew to the test.

On the ARA *San Luis* (S-32), its commander Frigate Captain Félix Rodolfo Bartolomé read the procedures and commented on them to his second-in-command: they were to be positioned east of Cape Horn, near the limit with the Pacific and wait there to attack the enemy fleet in case of an attack by the Chileans, they were especially to attack any ship that tried to approach the fleet through that sector.

Frigate Captain Eulogio Moya, commander of the ARA *Salta* (S-31), had just read his orders and had already given instructions to head towards the Wollaston Islands, east of Cape Horn, between 67° and 66°, sailing submerged at a speed of 18 knots.

The German-manufactured IKL.209-1200 submarines were, at that time, the most modern diesel-powered submarines in the world but they suffered from considerable flaws, as would be seen when they entered combat

during the Falklands campaign in 1982. They were equipped with a VM8/24 fire control computer for launching and guiding Telefunken SST-4 wire-guided torpedoes with a range of 25 kilometres, being able to attack three ships simultaneously. They also had active sonar, passive sonar, DUUG interceptor sonar, DUUX passive acoustic rangefinder, a spectral analyser, electromagnetic energy analyser, cavitation detector and two periscopes. Its lines had been designed to navigate long distances while submerged and in those conditions it could reach a speed of 20 to 22 knots. If these submarines had anything going against them, it was that, on the surface, the shape of their hulls made them very poor sailors, in addition to having little space inside and lacking bunks and seats for the crews. Argentina had successfully tested the IKL.209 during the 1975 manoeuvres, when they spent 50 days submerged, allowing their capabilities to be demonstrated and gave the naval High Command a high level of confidence.

During the voyage, one of the engines of ARA *San Luis* presented faults, a mishap that forced its commander to order it to surface and its mechanics to carry out an exhaustive review of the diesel system. The breakdown was serious and reduced the performance of the ship and the recharging of its batteries by 50 percent. A quick examination made it possible to determine the seriousness of the damage and despite the tireless efforts of the technicians on board, it could not be repaired. To achieve this, it was necessary to cut the hull, strip down the engine, replace it, and then weld it, work that could not be done on the high seas but only in dry dock. Captain Bartolomé reported the situation to the Naval Command and they ordered him to change the patrol zone, assigning him to the eastern mouth of the Strait of Magellan, where he arrived without incident

Two photos taken through the periscope of the submarine ARA *Santiago del Estero*. On the left, the Chilean submarine ACH *Simpson* and on the right, a Grumman S-2 Tracker of the Argentine Naval Aviation. (Histarmar Archives)

(Left) The helmsmen of the submarine ARA *Santiago del Estero*. Their long-bearded faces indicate long weeks in the ocean. (Right) The torpedo room of the same submarine. (Histarmar Archives)

on the morning of 18 December. Immediately afterwards, he was instructed to go to the Isla de los Estados where he was to meet the *Aracena*, a fishing vessel requisitioned by the Navy, to receive assistance from its personnel.

Between 18 and 19 December, ARA *Santa Fe* and ARA *Santiago del Estero* entered Chilean territorial waters, and on the night of the 19th they took up positions in their respective patrol areas.

On the morning of 20 December, the sonar of ARA *Santiago del Estero* detected a signal classified as a destroyer which was moving in a southerly direction. In order to identify the ship that produced the signal, Captain Sala ordered his boat to rise to periscope depth and instructed his men to occupy combat positions. Great was his surprise when he saw in his viewfinder the silhouette of a Balao-class submarine; it was ACH *Simpson* that, completely oblivious to the presence of the Argentine submarine, was moving on the surface, ignorant, like the rest of the Chilean Navy squadron, that enemy units were operating in Chilean territorial waters, east of Tierra del Fuego.

In view of this, the commander ordered a combat scramble and prepared the torpedoes for firing. The Chilean submarine had not detected the enemy presence and continued unperturbed, without evading or attacking and with some open deck hatches in the induction pipe section, which would have prevented a rapid dive. Immediately afterwards, the sonar operator noticed the sound of light propellers that seemed to be approaching the enemy submarine and warned his commander of this. ACH *Simpson* remained in sight of ARA *Santiago del Estero* for several minutes, making it possible to obtain a photograph that would become famous several years

later. Captain Sala notified the Fleet Command of the news and was ordered to remain in the area until further notice.

During ARA *Salta*'s journey to the patrol zone, when it was sailing off the Isla de los Estados, another event occurred that could also have triggered a tragedy. The submarine was recharging its batteries at snorkel depth when a Naval Aviation Grumman S-2E Tracker detected its presence and flying low, dropped several sonar buoys on it in order to identify it and fire an anti-submarine torpedo. ARA *Salta* quickly submerged and managed to escape while trying to establish contact with the Fleet Command to warn of its presence. The submarine continued its route submerged and a few hours later, once the danger was over, it reached the assigned area, rising again to snorkel depth to complete the recharging of its batteries. A very rough sea was encountered; something common in Cape Horn, with strong winds and waves up to six metres high that shook the ship with force and made it deviate from its route.

It was at that precise moment that the on-board systems detected an enemy radar that was monitoring the movements of the Argentine Sea Fleet from the ground. The fact did not go unnoticed by the crew, but, due to the strong waves, they were not detected. ARA *Salta* managed to escape and shortly after reached the assigned area, east of the Wollaston Islands, starting its patrol mission.

On 21 December, only hours before the attack, the submarine was recharging its batteries near Deceit Island, in the middle of the Chilean sea, when an extensive encrypted message arrived at the on-board communications centre that, due to bad weather conditions, was difficult to decipher. At that very moment, the captain ordered the officer on duty to take a look through the periscope and report

The fishing vessel *Aracena* of the private company Productos del Mar S.A. was requisitioned by the Argentine Navy as a support vessel for submarines. (Histarmar Archives)

if he observed anything unusual, and the crew was greatly surprised when, after a careful search, the officer reported that in front of ARA *Salta*, a submarine could be distinguished on the surface. Captain Moya rushed to take a look through the periscope and was thus able to distinguish the enemy unit and on deck, in front of the sail, at least two of its crew performing some type of task that he could not determine. It had to be a Balao-class because it was not possible to distinguish the characteristic dome of the Oberon-class and indeed, as it was later learned, it was ACH *Simpson*, the only operable boat that Chile had at the time. The commander ordered the battery recharging operation to be suspended, battle stations to be manned, and submerging to begin while the torpedo tubes were readied to launch two Mk.37 torpedoes.

No one could explain how such an easy, visual detection had been possible without the enemy noticing their presence, until someone commented that the sound of the old Balao-class recharging, with the four diesel engines running at full capacity, although diminished by the silencers, must have prevented its sonar operator from noticing the presence of ARA *Salta*, a flaw that would have been fatal if the war had broken out. Suddenly, the Argentine sonar operator noticed the sound of the enemy ship's ballast tanks venting and a few minutes later, the ship submerged and disappeared from sight, forcing Captain Moya to do the same in case they had been detected.

While S-31 was descending, the sound plotting table was set up to detect and predict mutual manoeuvres. Moments later the second-in-command talked to the commander over the intercom and told him they were ready to attack by launching the torpedoes. Since he got no immediate answer, he repeated the message. The commander responded but did not authorise the launch of the Mk.37 torpedoes since at that time they were not in Argentine territorial waters. Commander Moya had made the right decision because they were in Chilean territorial waters and the order not to shoot was in effect.

The tension became overwhelming and the silence extremely oppressive when the Argentine sonar operator reported the approach of a torpedo. The submarine began evasive manoeuvres and shortly after, the sonar operator was heard again, saying that the noise had disappeared and nothing could be perceived, words that restored tranquillity on board. Years later, Captain Scheihing himself stated that there was no torpedo launch whatsoever. After the moment of tension, it was possible to decipher the message received shortly before the encounter with ACH *Simpson*, through which the Fleet Command ordered the unit to withdraw to Isla de los Estados.

ARA *Santa Fe* patrolled the west mouth of the Strait of Magellan, between Cook Bay and Caroline Island, in the middle of the Chilean sea. It was submerged at a depth of 50 metres when, suddenly, its sonar noticed the growing sound of propellers that increased in power as the minutes passed. The operator alerted his commander, who ordered the alarm sounded, ordering the crew to occupy their combat stations and get the torpedo tubes ready to await the attack order. The officer in charge of the sonar spoke again, reporting this time that the hydrophonic noise had been transformed into a considerable squadron of at least 13 ships that were currently passing over them. It was the Chilean Sea Fleet that had abandoned its natural anchorages in the channel and gained open waters to put distance between its units and the Argentine air and naval bases, which represented a real threat. The operators on board were able to determine that they were cruisers and destroyers moving at cruising speed, without emitting signals, which was to say, without using the detection equipment on board the escort ships, a strange attitude, due to the risk that this implied.

It was evident that the Chileans were not looking for any submarine targets because even the most cautious of their officers did not consider the possibility that the Argentines were operating in the Chilean waters, much less in the western mouth of the strait. They also did not want to attract attention with their emissions because they spread over great distances and were easily detectable, which would leave them at the mercy of the enemy Naval Aviation.

ARA *Santa Fe* awaited the passage of the Chilean Squadron in silence and began to follow it slowly, with its weapons ready to fire as soon as hostilities broke out. The Chilean ships were extremely easy targets, their crews unaware of the threat lurking beneath the waters. Captain Manfrino understood that the enemy fleet was looking for open waters to prevent a possible air attack and considered that it did not constitute a threat to the Argentine forces, so he ordered them to take a position in an appropriate place and wait. At periscope depth and in a favourable tactical position, which would allow him to easily intercept the ships in case they turned in search of his own fleet, he slowly raised his communications antenna and, breaking radio silence, sent a report to the Naval Command giving an account of their position, that of the enemy, the number of ships that were moving, their speed and their course at the time of their detection. Argentina had located the enemy Sea Squadron.

5

IS IT ALL OVER?

Since the afternoon of 21 December, the Argentine Sea Fleet faced a fierce storm that had turned the sea extremely violent, with hurricane-force winds and waves that reached four metres in height. Under these conditions it was impossible to launch any attack operation, despite the high morale of the troops on board, especially among the elite troops, the tactical divers and the Marines who were waiting in the helicopters to carry out the diversionary attack on the islands of the channel.

Far away, on the mainland, the assault order was given, the battalions began advancing towards the border while at the air bases and improvised runways secretly built parallel to the mountain range, A-4B and A-4C Skyhawk attack aircraft, Canberra Mk.62 bombers and Mirage IIIEA fighters were on alert in order to take-off immediately for their targets.

That night, several Argentine regiments crossed the line of the border and entered Chilean territory without being detected. One of them penetrated 20 kilometres into Chile from the province of Santa Cruz and another did the same in Tierra del Fuego, without anyone realising it.

The Argentine Navy Sea Fleet, less than four hours from the point of 'no return' (6:30 p.m. on 22 December), in the midst of the terrible storm that was hitting the ships, began to slow down

On the night of 21-22 December, several Argentine regiments stationed on the southern border began to advance, entering Chilean territory. (Left) An infantry soldier posing with his FN MAG 60-20 machine gun. (Centre) Two soldiers posing with an Army Unimog truck. (Right) A column of Argentine Army trucks transporting supplies and ammunition to the border with Chile. (Ejército Argentino)

The massive mobilisation of the Argentine Army resulted in the sending of thousands of soldiers to different critical points on the border with Chile. (Ejército Argentino)

(Left) Argentine Army NCO Jorge Aguirre next to his re-engined M4 Sherman tank with a 105mm cannon. (Centre) Argentine gunners with a 40mm L60 anti-aircraft gun. (Right) Two soldiers from Company C of the 24th Infantry Regiment posing with a mortar. (Ejército Argentino)

The Argentine Army improvised an ammunition depot at the prison in the city of Ushuaia, in Tierra del Fuego. (Ejército Argentino)

and soon after began a slow turn, withdrawing from the area, in the direction of Isla de los Estados.

At the diplomatic level, the then President of Venezuela, Carlos Andrés Pérez, alerted the American President Jimmy Carter about the Argentine invasion. Carter in turn ordered his ambassador to the Vatican to implore Pope John Paul II to intervene to prevent the war. In an urgent meeting, out of protocol, the Pope listened carefully to the US diplomat and was shaken when he was told that Argentina had launched the attack and that he only had a few hours to stop it.

The Pope immediately agreed to be the mediator in the crisis between Argentina and Chilie and after the meeting ended, he sent for the Argentine ambassador to the Vatican, Rubén Víctor Manuel Blanco, and asked him to communicate urgently with his government to tell it that he was

Two Hughes 369 helicopters of the Argentine Air Force in the middle of the Andes mountain range near the border with Chile. (Dirección de Estudios Históricos de la Fuerza Aérea Argentina)

Two Dassault Mirage IIIEA fighters of the Argentine Air Force. (Dirección de Estudios Históricos de la Fuerza Aérea Argentina)

Argentine Air Force Douglas A-4B Skyhawks. (Dirección de Estudios Históricos de la Fuerza Aérea Argentina)

offering to mediate to reach a diplomatic solution. Without wasting a minute, Blanco went to the embassy and called Foreign Minister Pastor to convey the Pope's message and he, in turn, informed President Videla who quickly gave the order to call off the attack. Then, the Argentine high commands also realised that a war as they had planned it would not only not be a 'military walk over' but a bloody confrontation that would claim many victims on both sides. In addition, there was the threat from the government of the United States and the North Atlantic Treaty Organization countries that if Argentina invaded Chilean territory, it would be declared an aggressor country.

On the border with Chile, near Santa Cruz, an Argentine Air Force Hughes 369 helicopter crossed the border and landed a few metres in front of the vanguard of the forces that had entered enemy territory, to inform them that *Operación Soberanía* was cancelled, thus preventing the invasion of Chilean territory from continuing and returning the troops to their place of origin. In Tierra del Fuego, this operation was not necessary because, fortunately, radio contact was established in time.

In the morning of the 23 December, Pope John Paul II announced the visit of his personal delegate to both countries, in order to begin negotiations for a diplomatic agreement. That day, at 08:00, the military committee made up of Videla, the members of the Board and other high-ranking officials met in Buenos Aires, an opportunity in which the members of the hard-line wing of the Armed Forces harshly reproached the President for his attitude, for not understanding that the military machinery had been set in motion and it was very difficult to stop it.

A Naval Aviation Douglas A-4Q Skyhawk taking off from the aircraft carrier ARA *25 de Mayo*. (COAN)

(Left) A FACh F-5E fighter pilot. (Right) A Chilean Air Force Northrop F-5E Tiger II overflying the Andes mountain range. (FACh)

(Left) A few Chilean Air Force Hawker Hunters received a two-tone grey camouflage, more suitable for the southern territory. (Right) One Hunter with a light grey camouflage in the flight line together with others in their traditional British colour scheme. (FACh via Claudio Cáceres Godoy)

A FACh Cessna A-37B Dragonfly on a segment of the road that connects Puerto Montt with El Tepual, in southern Chile, on 28 December 1978. Seated on the wing, from left to right, Captain Michael Lambie, Lieutenant Luis Ili, Second Lieutenants Roberto Vargas and Marcelo Jara. (FACh)

(Left) Argentine Air Force Sikorsky S-61R/N and Bell 212 helicopters, all in tactical camouflage, at the Río Mayo Air Base in December 1978. (Comodoro (Ret.) Gabriel Pavlovcic). (Right) The only Sikorsky S-61R in service in the Air Force. (SOP (Ret.) Walter Bentancor)

On 26 December, Cardinal Antonio Samoré, personal envoy of Pope John Paul II, arrived in Buenos Aires and was received by the national authorities and the Apostolic Nuncio, Cardinal Pío Laghi. He did not know how hard a task Pope John Paul II had entrusted to him. Before and after the intervention of the Vatican, the pressure of the most warmongering military sector never yielded.

Two days later, the order to withdraw was given to the submarine force. ARA *Santiago del Estero* was ordered to go to the Isla de los Estados and await further instructions there. Its mission had lasted 36 days during which it sailed 4,012 nautical miles or 7,430km. ARA *Santa Fe* was also sent to the legendary island where Jules Verne had set one of his most famous novels, to make contact with the supply ship *Aracena*, in the waters of one of its coves. Arriving at the place,

(Left) Argentine soldiers in an M113 armoured personnel carrier. (Right) A column of Chilean Army vehicles going south. (Ejército Argentino & Ejército de Chile)

TABLE 2: Argentine Navy Submarine Force Campaign 1978[1]					
Submarine	Commander	Depart Puerto Belgrano Naval Base	Distance travelled	Hours submerged	Arrive Mar del Plata Naval Base
S-21 ARA *Santa Fe*	Frigate Captain A. Manfrino	8 December 1978	3,955nm	629	10 January 1979
S-22 ARA *Santiago del Estero*	Frigate Captain C. Sala	8 December 1978	4,012nm	708	13 January 1979
S-31 ARA *Salta*	Frigate Captain E. Moya	8 December 1978	4,573nm	750	16 January 1979
S-32 ARA *San Luis*	Frigate Captain F. Bartolomé	8 December 1978	3,384nm	876	16 January 1979

its captain saw ARA *San Luis* anchored next to the mother ship, after a campaign of 876 hours of navigation and 6,270 kilometres of travel. This is how the crews of both boats were able to bathe, relax, replenish their food supplies and prepare to spend Christmas and New Year there. Shortly after ARA *Salta* arrived, after 31 days of mission and 8,470 kilometres of travel, and there they remained until 16 January 1979, when the Force Command ordered them to return to their naval base in Mar del Plata.

It would appear that everyone in Chile and Argentina was calm and happy that the war had not broken out, except for the hard-line wing of the Argentine Armed Forces, who continued to show their displeasure and disagreement with what had happened. Although orders had already been received to stop the invasion, the troops of both countries continued to be deployed in the south, even spending the end of the year holidays in their positions. The majority returned to their bases of origin only during the month of January 1979.

6

FROM THE BATTLEFIELD TO THE FIELD OF DIPLOMACY

Perhaps the possibility of a war was over, but a long diplomatic dispute would begin that would last six years. Meanwhile Cardinal Antonio Samoré devoted himself fully to preventing war and accommodating the demands of both parties, within a dialogue of reasoning and compromise. Only when they reached an agreement on mediation and expressed their willingness to sign a principle of understanding, was the Papal Legate able to impose a paragraph in which he committed both countries to desist from the use of force, not to create situations of risk for peace and return to the status quo of 1977.

It was decided that Taranco Palace in Montevideo, headquarters of the Museum of Decorative Arts, would be the meeting place for the signing of the protocol, with the government of Uruguay officiating as host. But there were sectors in Argentina that opposed any settlement and tried to boycott the peace. Shortly before Foreign Minister Pastor left for the Uruguayan capital, the *Halcones* (Hawks) once again applied pressure. On 8 January 1979, the last serious pressure from the warmongering wing of the Army took place minutes before the take-off of the plane that would take Foreign Minister Pastor to Montevideo to sign the Montevideo Act, by which both countries accepted the mediation of the Pope, with his Chilean counterpart, Hernán Cubillos. Before Foreign Minister Pastor boarded the aircraft, an Army executive jet landed with General Luciano Benjamín Menéndez, who met with Pastor and ordered him not to travel to Montevideo. Pastor prevailed saying that he received his orders from President Videla and he left. Hours later, Argentina and Chile accepted Papal mediation, agreed to a non-aggression commitment and the gradual withdrawal of troops. The moral authority that the Pope possessed in both Catholic countries prevented the most warmongering sectors from rejecting the offer of mediation. Other battles began, but the war was behind them.

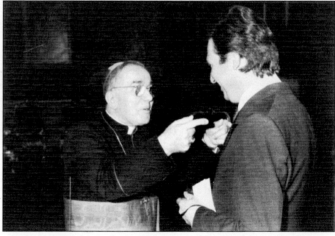

The representative of Pope John Paul II, Cardinal Antonio Samoré, had to make intense diplomatic efforts in both disputing countries to develop the mediation work of the Vatican. (Public Domain)

On 8 January, both Foreign Ministers signed the Act and thus committed themselves to seeking a peaceful solution to the border conflict, accepting Papal mediation.

Meanwhile, Chile wanted to level the balance in terms of military equipment so that between 1980 and 1981 additional war materiel was acquired, mainly from Israel and France. One-hundred-and-fifty Isherman M51 tanks (an Israeli modification of the M4 Sherman, with a Cummings diesel engine, new gearbox and improved suspension, plus a GIAT 105mm gun) were purchased from Israel, 30 AMX-30 tanks from France for the Army, and the FACh received 16 Dassault Mirage 50 fighters. During the 1980s, the Chilean Navy would also acquire fast attack missile craft from Israel and destroyers from the UK. In fact, Argentina was not left

(Left) The signing of the Act of Montevideo in the Taranco Palace. From left to right, Argentine Foreign Minister Carlos Washington Pastor, Cardinal Antonio Samoré and Chilean Foreign Minister Hernán Cubillos. (UPI). (Right) Until the last moment, General Luciano Benjamín Menéndez, representative of the hard-line of the Argentine military, tried in vain to ensure that this Act was not signed. (Public Domain)

behind either and continued to acquire air, naval and land weapons. The Argentine Air Force acquired more IAI M5 Dagger fighters, so its fleet reached 39 aircraft, plus 22 Dassault Mirage IIICJ/BJs, both models coming from Israel. Ten Dassault Mirage 5P Maras arrived from Peru, and three factory-new Boeing Vertol 308 Chinook helicopters. The Naval Aviation purchased 11 Embraer EMB-326GB Xavantes from Brazil, 14 Dassault Super Étendard fighter-bombers from France, and 10 Aermacchi MB-339A from Italy, and the Navy itself acquired Meko 360-class destroyers, Meko 140-class corvettes and a pair of TR1700-class submarines from Germany, fast PT Boats from Israel and more A69-class corvettes from France. The outbreak of the Falklands War in 1982, of course, greatly reduced Argentina's military capacity.

On 12 December 1980, Pope John Paul II presented his final proposal, which gave Chile all the islands in dispute, but Argentina would obtain limited rights to installations on the islands and would receive extensive navigation rights in the area. The Chilean inland water zone would be very small and it would have to cede economic exploitation, scientific research and environmental management rights to Argentina. Most of the disputed maritime territory would be Argentine, but Argentina would have to cede the same rights to Chile that it would receive in the sea under Chilean jurisdiction. That document did not satisfy Argentina because, in the first place, it did not recognise its sovereignty over the three islands and their surroundings and because, in addition, it gave it shared sovereignty over the 200 nautical miles of maritime exclusive economic zone that the British Court had awarded Chile in 1977. In the Holy Father's proposal, he recognised Argentine sovereignty in part of the channel, including Gable Island, and proposed that this vast maritime space become common to both nations, which could exploit it jointly.

That same day, the Argentine Foreign Minister boarded an *Aerolineas Argentinas* jet and headed back to Buenos Aires carrying a red folder in his briefcase containing the proposal. The next day, in Ezeiza, he boarded an official vehicle and from the airport went directly to the presidential residence of Olivos to deliver the document to Videla. The President fell silent when he read the text and immediately ordered Pastor to organise a meeting of the Working Group for Special Issues in the Palacio San Martín, for the first days of the following week.

On Monday, 15 December, at 08:00 a.m., the meeting took place, chaired by Dr. Federico Alberto del Río, a prestigious lawyer associated with the Navy with the rank of Frigate Captain, and the Director General of Information, Commodore Juan Carlos Cuadrado. While this was happening, Pastor personally received in his office on the first-floor other officials

Some of the Argentine Navy's acquisitions in the 1980s: Meko 360-class destroyers D-13 ARA *Sarandí* (top left) and D-11 ARA *La Argentina* (top right), Meko 140-class corvette P-42 ARA *Rosales* (bottom left) and TR1700-class submarine S-42 ARA *San Juan* (bottom right). (Histarmar Archives)

The complete text of the document signed by the chancellors of both countries stated the following:

Act of Montevideo, 8 January 1979, by which Chile and Argentina request the mediation of the Holy See in the Southern dispute and agree not to resort to the strength in their mutual relationships.

1. Invited by His Eminence Cardinal Antonio Samoré, Special Representative of His Holiness Pope John Paul II to carry out a peace mission accepted by the Governments of the Republic of Chile and the Republic of Argentina, the Foreign Ministers of both Republics, His Excellency Mr. Hernán Cubillos Sallato and His Excellency Mr. Carlos W. Pastor, who after analysing the dispute and taking into consideration;

2. That His Holiness John Paul II expressed in his message to the Presidents of both countries, on 11 December 1978, his conviction that a serene and responsible examination of the problem could make prevail "the demands of justice, of equity and prudence as a secure and stable foundation for the fraternal coexistence" of the two peoples;

3. That in his address to the College of Cardinals on 22 December 1978, the Holy Father recalled the concerns and wishes that he had already expressed for the search for a way to safeguard peace, strongly desired by the peoples of both countries;

4. That His Holiness Pope John Paul II expressed the desire to send a Special Representative of his to the capitals of the two States to obtain more direct and concrete information on the respective positions and to contribute to the achievement of a peaceful settlement of the controversy;

5. That a noble initiative was accepted by both governments;

6. That His Eminence Cardinal Antonio Samoré, designated for this mission of peace, has maintained, as of 26 December 1978, conversations with the highest Authorities of both countries and with his most immediate collaborators;

7. That on 1 January, when the "World Day of Peace" was celebrated by Pontifical order, His Holiness John Paul II referred to this delicate situation and hoped that the Authorities of both countries with vision of future, balance and courage, follow the paths of peace and the goal of a just and honourable solution can be reached as soon as possible;

8. Declare that both Governments hereby renew their appreciation to the Supreme Pontiff John Paul II for sending a Special Representative. They decide to use the offer of the Apostolic See to carry out a procedure and, considering giving all its value to this availability of the Holy See, they agree to ask it to act as a mediator in order to guide them in the negotiations and assist them in the search for a solution of the dispute for which both governments agreed to seek the method of peaceful solution that they considered most appropriate. To this end, the positions held and developed by the parties in the negotiations already carried out related to the Puerto Mont Act and the work to which it gave rise will be carefully taken into account;

9. Both Governments will notify the Holy See of the terms of the controversy as well as the background and criteria they deem pertinent, especially those considered in the course of the different negotiations, whose minutes, instruments and projects will be made available to them;

10. Both Governments declare that they have no objection to the Holy See, in the course of these steps, expressing ideas suggested by its careful studies on all the controversial aspects of the problem of the southern zone, with the aim of contributing to a peaceful settlement and acceptable to both parties. They declare their willingness to consider the ideas that the Holy See may express;

11. Consequently, with this Agreement, which is inscribed in the spirit of the norms contained in international instruments tending to preserve peace, both Governments join the concern of His Holiness John Paul II and consequently reaffirm their willingness to resolve through of mediation the pending issue.

Cardinal Antonio Samoré, Special Envoy of His Holiness John Paul II, upon receiving the request for mediation made by the Governments of the Republic of Chile and the Republic of Argentina, requests that said request be accompanied by the commitment that the two States will not resort to force in their mutual relations, they will carry out a gradual return to the military situation existing at the beginning of 1977 and they will refrain from adopting measures that could upset the harmony in any quarter.

The Foreign Ministers of both Republics, His Excellency Mr. Hernán Cubillos Sallato and His Excellency Mr. Carlos Washington Pastor, give their agreement on behalf of their respective Governments and sign with the same Cardinal six copies of identical tenor.

Given in Montevideo, on 8 January 1979.

Just in case: Between 1980 and 1981, Chile acquired 16 Dassault Mirage 50 fighters from France (FACh) (left top and bottom) and 150 M51 Isherman tanks from Israel (right top and bottom). (Ejército De Chile)

From 1979 to 1983, the Argentine Air Force acquired 22 Dassault Mirage IIICJ/BJs and more IAI M5 Dagger fighters from Israel (top left and right respectively). Also, 10 Dassault Mirage 5P Mara were purchased from Peru (bottom left) and three factory-new Boeing Vertol 308 Chinook helicopters (bottom right). (Dirección de Estudios Históricos de la Fuerza Aérea Argentina & Hernán Casciani collection)

specially summoned that morning, who were awaiting their turn in the nearby Green Room: Undersecretary for Foreign Relations Carlos Cavandoli, his counterpart for International Economic Relations, Raúl Curá, the Chief of Staff, Brigadier Carlos Bloomer Reeves, Guillermo Moncayo and Ricardo Etcheverry Boneo.

The group worked until 4:00 p.m., when Pastor met with his team, prior to the arrival of General Horacio Tomás Liendo, head

of the Joint Chiefs of Staff, with whom, at the end of the day, they decided to present their conclusions to Videla, General Viola his imminent successor in the Presidency of the Nation, and General Leopoldo Fortunato Galtieri, who would become Commander-in-Chief of the Army.

Argentina rejected the proposal outright and stood firm in its position. On the other hand, on 25 December 1980, Chile, accepted

Lieutenant General Leopoldo Fortunato Galtieri, appointed President of the Republic on 22 December 1981. After the disastrous military campaign in the Falklands War, he resigned as President on 18 June 1982. (Public Domain)

given by Pope John Paul II, addressed to the Vatican expressing its discontent because it did not deliver islands to Argentina and allowed a Chilean presence far into the Atlantic.

On 29 March 1981, General Videla was replaced by General Roberto Viola in the Presidency of the Republic. He was only in power until 11 December of that year and he was unable to prevail over the hard-line sectors of the Argentine armed forces. During his brief presidency there were again incidents with Chile. Without consulting with the political command, the Argentine Army arrested members of a supposed Chilean espionage network. The measure had repercussions in Chile, where two alleged Argentine spies were also arrested. In an escalation of tension, on 28 April 1981 General Leopoldo Fortunato Galtieri, Commander-in-Chief of the Argentine Army, closed the border with Chile, from north to south, without consulting the President or notifying the other branches of the armed forces. On 22 December 1981, General Leopoldo Fortunato Galtieri, until then head of the Army and one of the hardliners in the armed forces, assumed power in Argentina.

In January 1982, the new Argentine government denounced the Treaty on the Judicial Settlement of Controversies signed with Chile in 1972, which allowed each of the countries to access the International Court of Justice (ICJ) in The Hague in case of litigation, an option that Chile kept as the last resort. The Arbitration Award of 1977, favourable to Chile, supported actions in the field of international law, although they would be only symbolic since, as has been said, Argentina considered such a step a cause to start a war. The terms of the Treaty meant in practice that the final date to go to the ICJ was before the end of the year 1982 and that Chile had to decide between continuing with mediation or go to international law.

On 19 February 1982, six weeks before the start of the Falklands War, the Argentine tugboat ARA *Gurruchaga* anchored for three days on Deceit Island, despite Chilean protests and in violation of the Montevideo Act, which required refraining from carrying out acts that disturbed the harmony between both nations. All of these

the proposal, despite the fact that it lost 40km² of mainland, including the aforementioned Gable Island, and the 200 nautical miles to the southeast of the channel, 32,500km² of maritime area which became the exclusive economic zone of Argentina, setting the limit between the two nations at meridian 67° 15' 0".

After the Argentine rejection of the Papal proposal on 12 December 1980, the situation darkened again and the government only issued a note on 25 March 1981, two months after the deadline

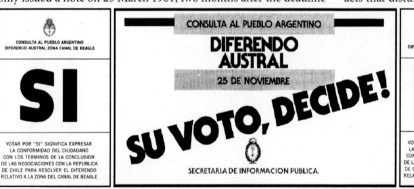
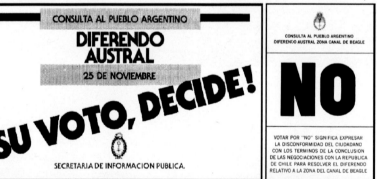

Ballots for the votes of the popular consultation of 25 November 1984, for the acceptance (SI) or rejection (NO) of the negotiations with Chile for the dispute in the Beagle area. (Public Domain)

(Left) From left to right, Argentine Foreign Minister Dante Caputo, Cardinal Agostino Casaroli and Chilean Foreign Minister Jaime del Valle, signing the Peace and Limits Treaty on 29 November 1984. (Right) Argentine Foreign Minister Dante Caputo (wearing glasses) signing the document in the presence of Pope John Paul II in the Vatican (right). (Public Domain)

obstacles had to be removed or at least lightened by Cardinal Antonio Samoré in order to maintain even the appearance of ongoing negotiations. In fact, there was no official progress in the negotiations, partly because Chile did not want to agree to give up the 1980 proposal it had already accepted.

On 2 April 1982, the Military Junta led by General Galtieri ordered the landing of Argentine forces on the Malvinas (Falklands) Islands, through *Operación Rosario* (Operation Rosary) starting the Falklands War against the United Kingdom, a subject that is outside of the scope of this volume. The Argentine debacle in that war caused the fall of the government of Lieutenant General Leopoldo Fortunato Galtieri and his replacement by Major General Reynaldo Benito Bignone on 1 July 1982,

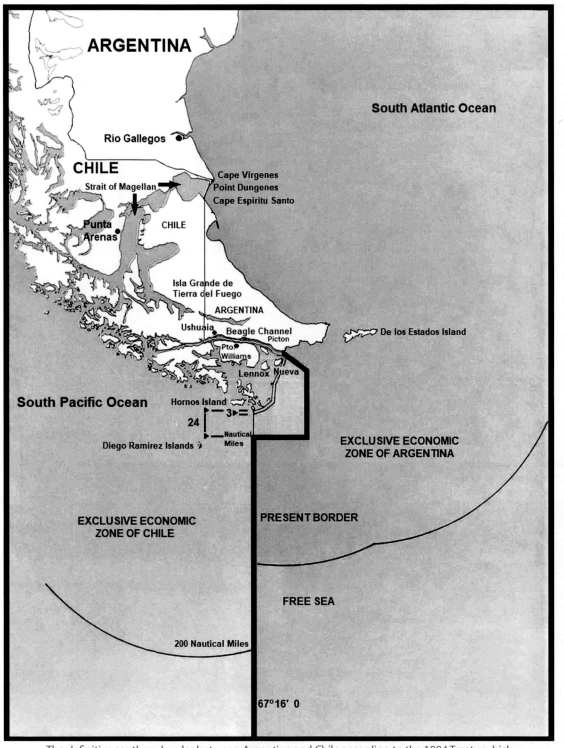

ARGENTINA

CHILE

Río Gallegos

Strait of Magellan

Cape Virgenes
Point Dungenes
Cape Espíritu Santo

South Atlantic Ocean

Punta Arenas

CHILE

Isla Grande de Tierra del Fuego

ARGENTINA

Ushuaia   Beagle Channel
Picton

De los Estados Island

Pto. Williams

Lennox Nueva

South Pacific Ocean

Hornos Island

24   3

Diego Ramirez Islands   Nautical Miles

EXCLUSIVE ECONOMIC ZONE OF ARGENTINA

EXCLUSIVE ECONOMIC ZONE OF CHILE

PRESENT BORDER

FREE SEA

200 Nautical Miles

67°16′ 0

The definitive southern border between Argentina and Chile according to the 1984 Treaty, which also included the territorial waters of both countries, as shown on the map. (Map by author)

Minister of Foreign Affairs. His position as the most powerful authority close to the Pope gave him a margin of manoeuvre that Samoré had not had.

On 30 October 1983, democratic elections were held in Argentina, the winner being the candidate of the Radical Civic Union (UCR) Raúl Ricardo Alfonsín, who assumed the Presidency of Argentina on 10 December of that year. Alfonsín's first objective was to reinsert Argentina into the concert of nations. To do this, he sought a quick solution to the problem of the Beagle. The negotiations were streamlined in such a way that, changing the method used until then, the negotiations between Ernesto Videla and Marcelo Delpech, heads of delegation from Chile and Argentina respectively, were held more in South America than in Rome.

Based on proposals from both governments, Cardinal Agostino Casaroli presented the last Papal proposal for mediation on 11 June 1984, but not before clarifying that a rejection of the proposal would mean for the Pope the unsuccessful end of mediation. Both parties accepted the proposal in principle.

In July of that year Santiago Benadava, a key figure in the Chilean delegation, met in The Hague with Julio Barbieri, the Argentine Ambassador to the Netherlands, during a visit on matters unrelated to the negotiations. Talking about the subject of the Beagle, they managed to find certain coincidences that they communicated to their respective governments, from which they obtained approval to continue exploring that path with the support of the mediator. The alternative was based on an Argentine renunciation of the islands and the facilities that the 1980 proposal granted, and Chile renounced the right to use Argentine waters and accepted only a small strip of territorial waters around the islands.

who governed only with the support of the Army. The defeat, the loss of prestige of the military leadership, the lack of support even among the armed forces and the brevity of his presidency prevented progress in this stage of the negotiations, with the exception of the extension of the 1972 Treaty on the Judicial Settlement of Controversies, agreed on 15 September 1982. The extension was only for matters of Papal mediation and could be resorted to only after the Pope had declared the mediation over and for a maximum period of six months.

Cardinal Antonio Samoré died at the age of 77 on 4 February 1983 and his position was taken by Cardinal Agostino Casaroli, Secretary of State of the Vatican, a position equivalent to that of

Southern Ice Field Litigation (still pending)

A pending dispute between Argentina and Chile is in the area of the southern ice field, as shown on the map. (Map by author)

The borders claimed by Argentine and Chile in the southern ice fields. (Map by author)

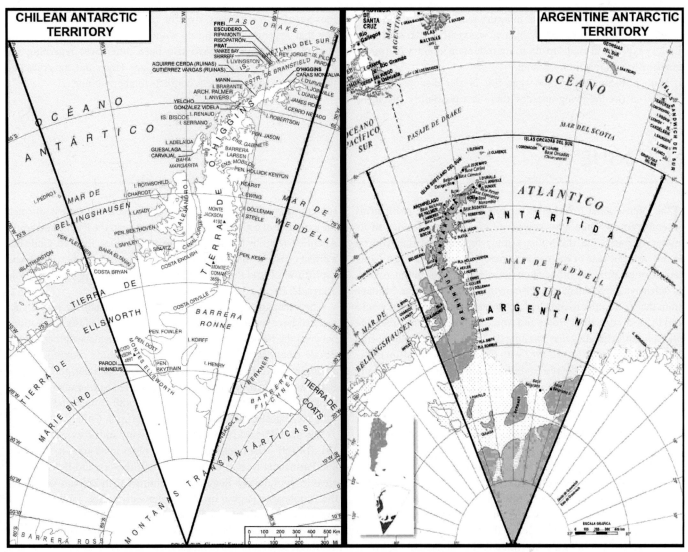

And as if everything related to borders in this volume were not enough, there is still the litigation of the Antarctic area of both countries, which practically overlap. (Public Domain)

The internal political situation in Argentina was undoubtedly the most determining factor in the negotiations. The military that governed the country during most of the mediation were divided between 'hardliners' and 'softliners'. Their actions were restricted by the fear of being replaced if they made shameful concessions to Chile. This atmosphere changed radically after the defeat in the Falklands War and the subsequent return to democracy. It was considered that before the Alfonsín government a solution to the conflict was unlikely. For Alfonsín it was a primary goal to recover foreign relations from the failure in which the National Reorganisation Process had left them. His government convened a popular consultation so that the citizens could support or reject the Pontifical text. The population, tired of years of war, violence and terror, voted favourably on 25 November 1984, with 82.6 percent (around 10.5 million people) voting for the 'YES' and 17.4 percent (2.2 million people) for the 'NO'. The popular consultation had the participation of 70 percent of the Argentine electorate.

Just four days later, on 29 November, the Treaty of Peace and Friendship between Argentina and Chile was signed in Rome by the respective Foreign Ministers Jaime del Valle of Chile and Dante Caputo of Argentina (see the appendix below for the full text of this Treaty). The Treaty was ratified in 1991 by Presidents Carlos Menem of Argentina and Patricio Aylwin of Chile, who considered the border conflict officially over.

But not everything was over, since there was still a dispute over the Laguna del Desierto area. In 1991 President Patricio Aylwin of Chile and President Carlos Menem of Argentina agreed to resort to international arbitration to solve the dispute. The court was established in Río de Janeiro on 15 December of that year, made up of the Colombian Rafael Nieto Navia, the Salvadoran Raynaldo Galindo Pohl, the Venezuelan Pedro Nikken, the Argentine Julio Barberis and the Chilean Santiago Benadava. On 21 October 1994, the court ruled in favour of Argentina, granting it the magnificent territory of Laguna del Desierto, which in 1965 had been the cause of a bloody dispute in which Chile suffered the worst part. The Santiago government complied with the decision immediately, resigning itself to the loss of 560km^2 of exuberant beauty and potential that had once belonged to it.

However, since 1998, the Southern Ice Field Litigation, that means the definitive establishment of the border from Mount Fitz Roy to Mount Daudet has remained pending. It seems to be a never-ending story. The zone was divided into two parts, Zone A, from Mount Murallón to Mount Daudet, and Zone B between Mount Fitz Roy and Mount Murallón. Supposedly the problem had been solved in 1902 but Argentina insisted on renegotiating, which was accepted by Chile. According to information that has been leaked, given the reserved nature of the matter, indicates that Zone A has already been delimited by mutual agreement between both countries, but

Zone B is still under discussion. In a very recent event, between 20 September and 5 October 2018, this area was visited by an Argentine military expedition made up of various mountain infantry regiments and the Mountain Military School.

Many Chileans think that when this border dispute is finally resolved in the following decades, there is a possibility, given the movement of the glaciers, that the country will be divided in two and that Argentina will end up with a beach on the Pacific Ocean. And even more, there have also been differences regarding the extended continental shelf south of Cape Horn and the Antarctic territories, so that, definitely, conflicts might continue …

EPILOGUE

The international isolation of the Chilean dictatorship, the arms embargo on Chile and Argentina's excessive confidence in its military capacity led the Military Junta to disregard the Arbitral Award without fear of the consequences of a war. Although Chile could not prevent Argentina from ignoring the Arbitration Award, its defensive deployment in 1978 convinced the Argentine Military Junta that taking the islands by force, even occupying them, would lead to more costs than profits and would expose it to unforeseeable risks, but unfortunately that was not taken into account in the events that took place from 2 April 1982 with the Argentine invasion of the Falklands Islands and the resounding defeat by British forces in June of the same year.

The consequences of that crisis were:

- Distraction from the internal problems of both nations by their political crimes.
- The exacerbated military spending that surely caused in part the economic disasters suffered by both countries.
- The entrenchment of both anti-democratic regimes.
- One or more generations on both sides of the border that grew up in fear and even hatred of their neighbour.
- This foreign policy led Argentina to the Falklands War and its consequences.
- Chile's direct intervention in the Falklands War, providing intelligence and logistical support to the British forces, was a preventive-defensive participation in the face of insinuations of future military actions.

Without threats of war or pressure, both countries accepted the Papal proposal that gave Argentina most of the exclusive economic zone granted by the disputed islands in exchange for Argentina's acceptance of the Arbitral Award of 1977. However, Chile achieved the *de facto* bioceanity and gained an outlet to the Atlantic Ocean, something that was not recognised by this country since it affirmed the existence of a natural delimitation between the Pacific and South Atlantic oceans by the arc of the Austral Antilles. Even so, Chile has a direct coastline of about 18km long on the Atlantic between Cabo Espíritu Santo and Punta Catalina in the north of the Isla Grande de Tierra del Fuego.

The exchange of navigation rights and the stability of the pact reached have made it possible to achieve great solidity in relations between the two countries and has favoured the development of the Beagle Channel region and made possible some progress that in 1978 seemed impossible. In homage to the mediator, the Puyehue Pass was renamed Cardenal Antonio Samoré International Pass. It is the second most important pass between both nations and connects Villa La Angostura in Argentina and Osorno in Chile.

During 1977 and 1978, the Chilean Army and Navy laid a total of 181,814 anti-personnel and anti-tank mines in 89 areas in the Arica and Parinacota Region on the borders with Peru and Bolivia, eight areas in the Tarapacá Region on the border with Bolivia, 66 areas in the Antofagasta Region on the border with Bolivia and Argentina, two areas in the Valparaíso Region and one area in the Metropolitan Region of Santiago, both on the border with Argentina. In the Southern Region of Magallanes, there were 28 areas on the border with Argentina. Specifically, in the Beagle Channel region, there were around 3,500 mines installed by the Chilean Navy in 17 fields distributed as follows: five on Picton Island, eight on Nueva Island, two on Deceit Island, one on Freycinet Island and one on the island of Horn. The types laid were: PRB M-35 (Belgium), M2A4, M14 NA, M16 NA and M16A1 (USA), and Cardoen Model I/II, M-178 and FAMAE P78, series F2 and T78-F2 (Chile) anti-personnel mines, and PRB M3A1 (Belgium), M15 (USA) and FAMAE F2 and 77F3 (Chile) anti-tank mines.

In recent years, however, the Marine Infantry Detachment No.4 *Cochrane*, based in Punta Arenas, proceeded to deactivate the anti-

Mute witnesses that more than 40 years ago Argentina and Chile were about to be at war in the Beagle area. (Histarmar Archives)

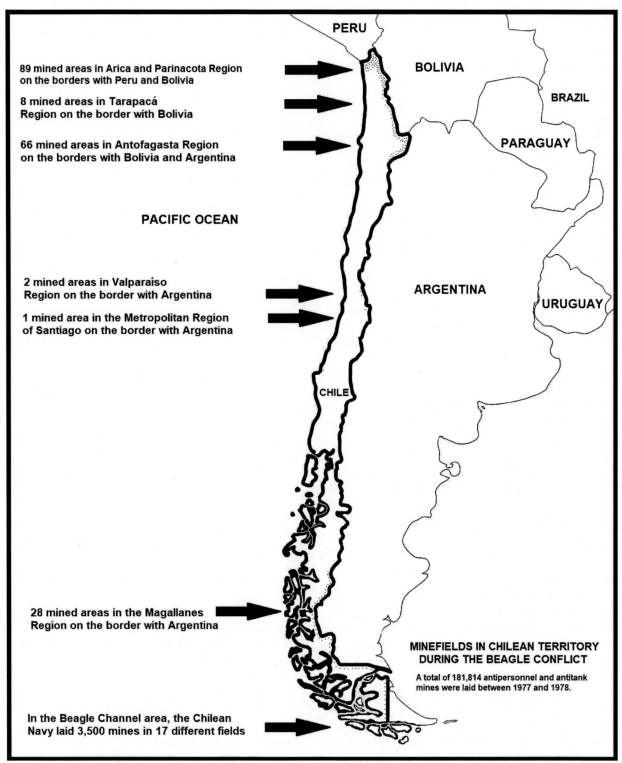

89 mined areas in Arica and Parinacota Region on the borders with Peru and Bolivia

8 mined areas in Tarapacá Region on the border with Bolivia

66 mined areas in Antofagasta Region on the borders with Bolivia and Argentina

PACIFIC OCEAN

2 mined areas in Valparaíso Region on the border with Argentina

1 mined area in the Metropolitan Region of Santiago on the border with Argentina

PERU

BOLIVIA

BRAZIL

PARAGUAY

ARGENTINA

URUGUAY

CHILE

28 mined areas in the Magallanes Region on the border with Argentina

MINEFIELDS IN CHILEAN TERRITORY DURING THE BEAGLE CONFLICT

A total of 181,814 antipersonnel and antitank mines were laid between 1977 and 1978.

In the Beagle Channel area, the Chilean Navy laid 3,500 mines in 17 different fields

Map showing the minefields on Chilean territory during the Beagle Crisis in 1977–1978. (Map by author)

personnel mines that were still in place on the above-mentioned islands, a process that was completed in 2018, at least in that area in the south of the country. It must be considered that the laying of minefields was not only carried out in the Magellan region in southern Chile, but also in the north, in Arica and Parinacota, Tarapacá and Antofagasta, border regions with Bolivia, Peru and Argentina, as well as the Metropolitan Region and Valparaíso in central Chile, areas that are being cleared by the Chilean Army through its Humanitarian Demining Units (UDH). By the year 2020, 96.41 percent of mined territories had been cleared, having destroyed 179,815 mines in the process.

In what was the hot zone of this conflict of 1978, a visitor can still see some vestiges of the war that fortunately did not take place between Argentina and Chile. When exploring the area of Ushuaia, Argentina, or Puerto Williams, Puerto Navarino or Puerto Toro in Chile, it is still possible to see certain silent witnesses of that time, Bofors, Oto Melara or Krupp guns, in their original emplacements, aiming at enemy targets across the Beagle Channel …

APPENDICES

APPENDIX I
The 1984 Peace and Friendship Treaty Between Argentina and Chile

In the name of Almighty God,

The Government of the Republic of Chile and the Government of the Argentine Republic,

Recalling that on 8 January 1979, they requested the Holy See to act as Mediator in the dispute raised in the southern zone, in order to guide them in the negotiations and assist them in the search for a solution; and that they required their valuable help to establish a delimitation line, which would determine the respective jurisdictions to the East and West of that line, from the end of the existing delimitation;

Convinced that it is the unavoidable duty of both Governments to give expression to the peace aspirations of their Peoples;

Bearing in mind the Boundary Treaty of 1881, the unshakeable foundation of the relations between the Argentine Republic and the Republic of Chile, and its complementary and declaratory instruments;

Reiterating the obligation to always settle all their disputes by peaceful means and to never resort to the threat or use of force in their mutual relations;

Encouraged by the purpose of intensifying economic cooperation and physical integration of their respective countries;

Taking especially into consideration the "Proposal of the Mediator, suggestion and advice," of 12 December 1980;

Testifying, on behalf of their Peoples, the thanks to His Holiness Pope John Paul II for his enlightened efforts to achieve a solution to the dispute and strengthen friendship and understanding between both Nations;

They have resolved to celebrate the following Treaty, which constitutes a compromise, for which purpose they come to designate as their Representatives:

His Excellency the President of the Republic of Chile to Mr. Jaime del Valle Alliende, Minister of Foreign Affairs;

His Excellency the President of the Argentine Republic to Mr. Dante Mario Caputo, Minister of Foreign Affairs and Worship; who have agreed as follows:

Article 1. The High Contracting Parties, responding to the fundamental interests of their Peoples, solemnly reiterate their commitment to preserve, strengthen and develop their ties of unalterable peace and perpetual friendship. The Parties will hold periodic consultation meetings in which they will especially examine any fact or situation that is likely to alter the harmony between them, they will try to prevent a discrepancy in their points of view from giving rise to a controversy and they will suggest or adopt concrete measures tending to maintain and strengthen the good and relations between both countries.

Article 2. The Parties confirm their obligation to refrain from directly or indirectly resorting to any form of threat or use of force and from adopting any other measure that may disturb harmony in any sector of their mutual relations. They also confirm their obligation to always and exclusively settle all controversies by peaceful means, of any nature, that for whatever reason have arisen or may arise between them, in accordance with the following provisions.

Article 3. If a controversy arises, the Parties will adopt the appropriate measures to maintain the best general conditions of coexistence in all areas of their relations and to prevent the controversy from worsening or being prolonged.

Article 4. The Parties will strive to achieve the solution of any dispute between them through direct negotiations, carried out in good faith and in a spirit of cooperation. If, in the opinion of both Parties or one of them, direct negotiations do not reach a satisfactory result, either Party may invite the other to submit the dispute to a means of peaceful settlement chosen by mutual agreement.

Article 5. In the event that the Parties, within the period of four months from the invitation referred to in the previous article, do not agree on another means of peaceful settlement and on the term and other modalities of its application, or that once said agreement has been reached, the solution is not reached for any reason, the conciliation procedure stipulated in Chapter I of Annex No. 1 will be applied.

Article 6. If both Parties or one of them have not accepted the settlement terms proposed by the Conciliation Commission within the period set by its President, or if the conciliation procedure fails for any reason, both Parties or either of them may submit the dispute to the procedure arbitration established in Chapter II of Annex No. 1. The same procedure will be applied when the Parties, in accordance with Article 4, choose arbitration as a means of resolving the dispute, unless they agree to other rules. Issues that have been the subject of final arrangements between the Parties may not be renewed under this article. In such cases, the arbitration will be limited exclusively to the questions that arise about the validity, interpretation and fulfilment of said agreements.

Maritime Delimitation

Article 7. The limit between the respective sovereignties over the sea, soil and subsoil of the Argentine Republic and the Republic of Chile in the Southern Zone Sea from the end of the existing delimitation in the Beagle Channel, that is, the point set by the coordinates 55° 07'.3 South latitude and 66° 25'.0 West longitude, will be the line that joins the points indicated below: From the point set by the coordinates 55° 07'.3 South latitude and 66° 25'.0 West longitude (point A), the delimitation will follow a loxodromic line to the Southeast to a point located between the coasts of the Island Nueva and Isla Grande de Tierra del Fuego, whose coordinates are 55° 11'.0 South latitude and 66° 04'.7 West longitude (point B); from there it will continue in a south-easterly direction at an angle of 45 degrees, measured at said point B, and will continue to the point whose coordinates are 55° 22', 9 South latitude and 65°43',6 West longitude (point C); it will continue directly towards the South by said meridian until the parallel 56° 22'.8 of South latitude (point D); from there it will continue along that parallel located 24 nautical miles south of the southernmost tip of Hornos Island, towards the west until its intersection with the meridian corresponding to the southernmost point of said Hornos Island at coordinates 56° 22'.8 South latitude and 67° 16'.0 West longitude (point E); from there the limit will continue towards the South to the point whose coordinates are 58° 21'.1 South latitude and 67° 16'.0 West longitude (point F). The previously described maritime delimitation line is represented in the attached Chart No. I. The Exclusive Economic Zones of the Argentine Republic and the Republic of Chile will extend respectively to the East and West of the limit thus described. To the South of the final point of the limit (point F), the Exclusive Economic Zone of the Republic of Chile will extend, up to the distance permitted by international law, to the West of the meridian 67° 16'.0 West longitude, demarcating the East with the high seas.

Article 8. The Parties agree that, in the space between Cape Horn and the easternmost point of Isla de los Estados, the legal effects of the territorial sea are limited, in their mutual relations, to a strip of three nautical miles measured from their respective baselines. In the space indicated in the previous paragraph, each Party may invoke the maximum width of territorial sea vis-à-vis third States that international law allows.

Article 9. The Parties agree to call the maritime space that has been the object of delimitation in the two previous articles the "Southern Zone Sea".

Article 10. The Republic of Argentina and the Republic of Chile agree that in the eastern terminus of the Strait of Magellan, determined by Punta Dungenes in the North and Cabo del Espíritu Santo in the South, the limit of their respective sovereignties shall be the straight line joining the "Hito Ex-Dungenes Beacon", located at the end of said geographical feature, and the "Hito I Cabo del Espíritu Santo" in Tierra del Fuego. The previously described delimitation line is represented in the attached Letter No. II. The sovereignty of the Argentine Republic and the sovereignty of the Republic of Chile over the sea, soil and subsoil will extend, respectively, to the East and West of said limit. The delimitation agreed herein in no way alters what is established in the 1881 Boundary Treaty, according to which the Strait of Magellan is neutralised in perpetuity and its free navigation is ensured for the flags of all nations in the terms indicated in its Article V. The Argentine Republic undertakes to maintain, at any time and under all circumstances, the right of ships of all flags to navigate expeditiously and without obstacles through its territorial waters to and from the Strait of Magellan.

Article 11. The Parties mutually recognise the straight baselines they have drawn in their respective territories.

Economic Cooperation and Physical Integration

Article 12. The Parties agree to create a permanent Binational Commission in order to intensify economic cooperation and physical integration. The Binational Commission will be in charge of promoting and developing initiatives, among others, on the following topics: global system of land links, mutual authorisation of ports and free zones, land transportation, air navigation, electrical interconnections and telecommunications, exploitation of natural resources, protection of the environment and tourism complementation. Within six months of the entry into force of this Treaty, the Parties will constitute the Binational Commission and will establish its regulations.

Article 13. The Republic of Chile, in exercise of its sovereign rights, grants the Argentine Republic the navigation facilities specified in Articles 1 to 9 of Annex No. 2. The Republic of Chile declares that third-flag vessels may navigate without obstacles along the routes indicated in Articles 1 and 8 of Annex No. 2, subject to the pertinent Chilean regulations. Both Parties agree

to the Navigation, Piloting and Pilotage regime in the Beagle Channel that is specified in the aforementioned Annex No. 2, Articles 11 to 16. The stipulations on navigation in the southern zone contained in this Treaty supersede any previous agreement on the matter that may exist between the Parties.

Final clauses

Article 14. The Parties solemnly declare that this Treaty constitutes the complete and final solution of the issues to which it refers. The limits indicated in this Treaty constitute a definitive and immovable boundary between the sovereignties of the Argentine Republic and the Republic of Chile. The Parties undertake not to submit claims or interpretations that are incompatible with the provisions of this Agreement.

Article 15. Articles 1 to 6 of this Treaty shall be applicable in the Antarctic territory. The other provisions will not affect in any way nor can they be interpreted in the sense that they may affect, directly or indirectly, the sovereignty, rights, legal positions of the Parties, or the delimitations in Antarctica or in its adjacent maritime spaces, including the soil and the subsoil.

Article 16. Accepting the generous offer of the Holy Father, the High Contracting Parties place this Treaty under the moral protection of the Holy See.

Article 17. They form an integral part of this Treaty:

a) Annex No. 1 on the Conciliation and Arbitration procedure, which consists of 41 articles;

b) Annex No. 2 relating to navigation, which consists of 16 articles; and the Letters referred to in articles 7 and 10 of the Treaty and in Articles 1, 8 and 11 of Annex No. 2.

References to this Treaty are also understood to be made to their respective Annexes and Letters.

Article 18. This Treaty is subject to ratification and shall enter into force on the date of the exchange of the instruments of ratification.

Article 19. This Treaty shall be registered in accordance with Article 102 of the Charter of the United Nations.

In witness whereof, they sign and seal this Treaty in six copies of the same tenor, of which two will remain in the possession of the Holy See and the others in the possession of each of the Parties.

Done in Vatican City on the Twenty-Ninth of November, one thousand nine hundred and eighty-four.

Dante Mario Caputo   Jaime del Valle Alliende
Before me Cardinal Agostino Casaroli

ANNEX NO. 1

CHAPTER I
Conciliation procedure provided for in Article 5 of the Treaty of Peace and Friendship

Article 1. Within a period of six months from the entry into force of this Agreement, the Parties shall establish a Permanent Argentine-Chilean Conciliation Commission, hereinafter "the Commission". The Commission will consist of three members. Each of the Parties shall appoint a member, who may be chosen from among their nationals. The third member, who will act as Chairman of the Commission, will be elected by both Parties among nationals of third States who do not have their habitual residence in their territory or are not in their service. Members will be appointed for a term of three years and may be re-elected. Each of the Parties may proceed at any time to replace the member appointed by it. The third member may be replaced during his term by agreement between the Parties. Vacancies caused by death or for any other reason will be filled in the same way as the initial appointments, within a period not exceeding three months. If the appointment of the third member of the Commission cannot be made within a period of six months from the entry into force of this Agreement or within a period of three months from the occurrence of a vacancy, as the case may be, either Party may request the Holy See to make the designation.

Article 2. In the situation provided for in Article 5 of the Treaty of Peace and Friendship, the controversy shall be submitted to the Commission by written request, whether joint or separate, of the Parties, or of one of them, addressed to the President of the Commission. The request shall summarily indicate the object of the dispute. If the request is not joint, the appellant Party shall immediately notify the other Party.

Article 3. The written request or requests by means of which the controversy is submitted to the Commission shall contain, to the extent possible, the designation of the Delegate or Delegates by whom the Party or Parties from which the requests emanate will be represented in the Commission. It will be the responsibility of the President of the Commission to invite the Party or Parties that have not designated a Delegate to proceed with their prompt designation.

Article 4. Once a dispute has been submitted to the Commission, and for its sole purpose, the Parties may designate, by mutual agreement, two more members to integrate it. The presidency of the Commission will continue to be exercised by the previously designated third member.

Article 5. If, at the time the dispute is submitted to the Commission, any of the members appointed by a Party is not in a position to fully participate in the conciliation procedure, that Party must replace him as soon as possible for the sole purpose of said conciliation. At the request of either Party, or on his own initiative, the President may require the other to proceed with that substitution. If the President of the Commission is not in a position to fully participate in the conciliation procedure, the Parties must replace him by mutual agreement, as soon as possible, by another person for the sole purpose of said conciliation. In the absence of agreement, either Party may request the Holy See to make the designation.

Article 6. Upon receipt of a request, the President will set the place and date of the first meeting and will convene the members of the Commission and the Delegates of the Parties. At the first meeting, the Commission shall appoint its Secretary, who may not be a national of any of the Parties or have permanent residence in their territory or be at their service. The Secretary will remain in office for the duration of the conciliation. At the same meeting, the Commission will determine the procedure to which the conciliation will have to be adjusted.

Article 7. The Parties will be represented in the Commission by their Delegates; they may also be assisted by advisers and experts appointed by them for these purposes and request the testimonies they deem appropriate. The Commission will have the power to request explanations from the Delegates, advisers and experts of the Parties, as well as from other people it deems useful.

Article 8. The Commission will meet in the place that the Parties agree and, in the absence of agreement, in the place designated by its President.

Article 9. The Commission may recommend to the Parties measures tending to prevent the controversy from worsening or the conciliation from becoming more difficult.

Article 10. The Commission may not meet without the presence of all its members. Unless otherwise agreed by the Parties, all decisions of the Commission shall be taken by majority vote of its members. In the respective minutes it will not be stated if the decisions have been taken unanimously or by majority.

Article 11. The Parties shall facilitate the work of the Commission and shall provide it, to the greatest extent possible, with all useful documents or information. Likewise, they will allow them to proceed in their respective territories to summon and hear witnesses or experts and to carry out visual inspections.

Article 12. Upon completion of the examination of the dispute, the Commission will endeavour to define the terms of a settlement that can be accepted by both Parties. The Commission may, for this purpose, proceed to exchange points of view with the Delegates of the Parties, whom it may hear jointly or separately. The terms proposed by the Commission shall only have the nature of recommendations submitted to the consideration of the Parties in order to facilitate a mutually acceptable arrangement. The terms of said arrangement will be communicated, in writing, by the President to the Delegates of the Parties, who will be invited to let him know, within the term set, whether or not the respective Governments accept the proposed arrangement. When making the aforementioned Communication, the President will personally present the reasons that, in the Commission's opinion, advise the Parties to accept the settlement. If the controversy deals exclusively with issues of fact, the Commission will limit itself to investigating them and will record its conclusions in a record.

Article 13. Once both Parties accept the arrangement proposed by the Commission, a record will be drawn up in which said arrangement will be recorded, which will be signed by the President, the Secretary of the Commission and the Delegates. A copy of the minutes, signed by the President and the Secretary, will be sent to each of the Parties.

Article 14. If both Parties or one of them do not accept the proposed settlement and the Commission deems it superfluous to try to reach agreement on different terms of settlement, a record will be drawn up signed by the President and the Secretary, in which, without reproducing the terms of the proposed settlement, it will be stated that the Parties could not be reconciled.

Article 15. The work of the Commission must finish within a period of six months counted from the day the controversy was submitted to it, unless the Parties agree otherwise.

Article 16. No statement or communication by the Delegates or the members of the Commission on the merits of the controversy will be recorded in the minutes of the sessions, unless the Delegate or the member from whom it emanates consents. On the contrary, the written or oral expert reports and the minutes related to the visual inspections and witness statements will be attached to the minutes of the sessions, unless the Commission decides otherwise.

Article 17. Authenticated copies of the minutes of the sessions and their annexes will be sent to the Delegates of the Parties through the Secretary of the Commission, unless the Commission decides otherwise.

Article 18. The work of the Commission shall not be made public except by virtue of a decision made by the Commission with the consent of both Parties.

Article 19. No admission or proposal formulated during the course of the conciliation procedure, either by one of the Parties or by the Commission, may prejudge or affect, in any way, the rights or claims of one or the other Party in the event that the conciliation procedure does not prosper. In the same way, the acceptance by a Party of a draft settlement formulated by the Commission will not imply, in any way, acceptance of the factual or legal considerations on which said settlement could be based.

Article 20. Once the work of the Commission is finished, the Parties will consider whether to authorise the total or partial publication of the documentation related to them. The Commission may address a recommendation to this effect.

Article 21. During the work of the Commission, each one of its members will receive a pecuniary compensation whose amount will be fixed by common agreement by the Parties, which will defray it by halves. Each of the Parties will pay its own expenses and half of the common expenses of the Commission.

Article 22. At the end of the conciliation, the President of the Commission will deposit all the documentation related to it in the archives of the Holy See, maintaining the reserved nature of said documentation, within the limits indicated in articles 18 and 20 of this Annex.

CHAPTER II
Arbitration Procedure provided for in Article 6 of the Treaty of Peace and Friendship

Article 23. The Party that intends to resort to arbitration will inform the other by written notification. In the same communication, it will request the constitution of the Arbitral Tribunal, hereinafter "the Tribunal", it will summarily indicate the object of the controversy, it will mention the name of the arbitrator chosen by it to integrate the Tribunal and it will invite the other Party to enter into a commitment or agreement. The requested Party shall cooperate in the constitution of the Tribunal and in the execution of the compromise.

Article 24. Unless otherwise agreed by the Parties, the Arbitral Tribunal shall be made up of five members appointed in their personal capacity. Each of the Parties shall appoint a member, who may be their national. The other three members, one of whom will be President of the Tribunal, will be chosen by mutual agreement among nationals of third States. These three arbitrators must be of different nationalities, not have habitual residence in the territory of any of the Parties or be at their service.

Article 25. If all the members of the Tribunal have not been appointed within a period of three months from the receipt of the communication provided for in Article 23, the appointment of the missing members will be made by the Government of the Swiss Confederation at the request of Whatever of the parties. The President of the Tribunal will be designated by common agreement by the Parties within the term provided in the preceding paragraph. In the absence of agreement such designation shall be made by the Government of the Swiss Confederation at the request of either Party. Once all the members have been appointed, the President will summon them to a session in order to declare the Tribunal constituted and adopt the other agreements that are necessary for its operation. The session will be held in the place, day and time indicated by the President and the provisions of Article 34 of this Annex will be applicable to it.

Article 26. Vacancies that may occur due to death, resignation or any other cause will be covered in the following way:

• If the vacancy is that of a member of the Tribunal appointed by only one of the Parties, said Party will fill it as soon as possible and, in any case, within thirty days from the date the other Party invites it in writing to do so.

• If the vacancy is that of one of the members of the Tribunal appointed by mutual agreement, the vacancy will be filled within a period of sixty days from the date that one of the Parties invites the other in writing to do so.

• If within the terms indicated in the preceding paragraphs the aforementioned vacancies have not been filled, either Party may request the Government of the Swiss Confederation to proceed to do so.

Article 27. In the event that the commitment to submit the dispute to the Tribunal is not reached within a period of three months from its constitution, either Party may submit the dispute to the Tribunal by written request.

Article 28. The Tribunal shall adopt its own procedural rules, without prejudice to those that the Parties may have agreed upon in the compromise.

Article 29. The Tribunal will have powers to interpret the agreement and rule on its own jurisdiction.

Article 30. The Parties will offer their collaboration to the work of the Tribunal and will provide it with all the documents, facilities and useful information. Likewise, they will allow him to proceed in their respective territories, to the summons and hearing of witnesses or experts and to the practice of visual inspections.

Article 31. The Tribunal shall have the power to order provisional measures aimed at safeguarding the rights of the Parties.

Article 32. When one of the Parties in the controversy does not appear before the Court or refrains from defending its case, the other Party may request the Court to continue the proceedings and issue a sentence. The circumstances of one of the Parties being absent or not appearing will not be an obstacle to carry out the proceedings or to issue a sentence.

Article 33. The Tribunal will decide in accordance with international law, unless the Parties have provided otherwise in the agreement.

Article 34. The decisions of the Tribunal shall be adopted by a majority of its members. The absence or abstention of one or two of its members will not be an impediment for the Tribunal to meet or reach a decision. In the event of a tie, the President's vote will decide.

Article 35. The judgement of the Court will be motivated. It will mention the names of the members of the Court who have participated in its adoption and the date on which it was issued. Every member of the Tribunal shall have the right to have their separate or dissenting opinion added to the judgement.

Article 36. The judgement shall be binding on the Parties, final and unappealable. Its fulfilment is delivered to the honour of the Signatory Nations of the Treaty of Peace and Friendship.

Article 37. The judgement must be executed without delay in the manner and within the time limits indicated by the Court.

Article 38. The Court will not cease its functions until it has declared that, in its opinion, material and complete execution of the judgement has been given.

Article 39. Unless the Parties agree otherwise, the disagreements that arise between the Parties regarding the interpretation or the mode of execution of the arbitral award may be submitted by any of the Parties to the decision of the Tribunal that issued it. For this purpose, any vacancy that occurs on the Tribunal will be filled in the manner established in Article 26 of this Annex.

Article 40. Any of the Parties may request the review of the judgement before the Court that issued it, provided that it is deducted before the deadline for its execution expires, and in the following cases:

1. If a sentence has been handed down by virtue of a false or adulterated document.
2. If the sentence has been in whole or in part a consequence of a factual error, resulting from the proceedings or documents of the case.

For this purpose, any vacancy that occurs on the Tribunal will be filled in the manner established in Article 26 of this Annex.

Article 41. Each one of the members of the Tribunal will receive pecuniary compensation whose amount will be fixed by common agreement with the Parties, which will pay for it by halves.

Each of the Parties shall pay its own expenses and half of the common expenses of the Tribunal.

Jaime del Valle Alliende   Dante Mario Caputo

ANNEX NO. 2

Navigation between the Strait of Magellan and Argentine ports in the Beagle Channel, and vice versa.

Article 1. For maritime traffic between the Strait of Magellan and Argentine ports in the Beagle Channel, and vice versa, through Chilean internal waters, Argentine ships will enjoy navigation facilities exclusively for passage through the following route: Magdalena Channel, Cockburn Channel, Brecknock Pass or Ocasión Channel, Whaling Channel, O'Brien Channel, Timbales Pass, Northwest Arm of the Beagle Channel and Beagle Channel up to meridian 68° 36' 38.5" West longitude and vice versa. The description of the mentioned route is indicated in the attached Letter N° III.

Article 2. The passage will be carried out with a Chilean pilot, who will act as technical adviser to the Commander or Captain of the ship. For the timely appointment and boarding of the pilot, the Argentine authority will notify the Commander-in-Chief of the Third Chilean Naval Zone, at least forty-eight hours in advance, the date on which the ship will begin navigation. The pilot will exercise his function between the point whose geographical coordinates are: 54° 02'.8 South latitude and 70° 57'.9 West longitude and the meridian 68° 36' 38",5 West longitude in the Beagle Channel. When navigating to or from the eastern mouth of the Strait of Magellan, the pilot will embark or disembark at the Bahía Posesión Pilot Post in the Strait of Magellan. When navigating to or from the western mouth of the Strait of Magellan, you will embark or disembark at the corresponding

point indicated in the previous paragraph. Will be driven to and from the aforementioned points by a Chilean means of transport. When sailing to or from Argentine ports in the Beagle Channel, the pilot will embark or disembark in Ushuaia, and will be driven from Puerto Williams to Ushuaia or from the latter port to Puerto Williams by an Argentine means of transport. Merchant ships must pay the pilotage expenses established in the Tariff Regulation of the General Directorate of the Maritime Territory and Merchant Navy of Chile.

Article 3. The passage of Argentine ships will be continuous and uninterrupted. In case of detention or anchoring due to force majeure on the route indicated in Article 1, the Commander or Captain of the Argentine ship will inform the nearest Chilean naval authority of the fact.

Article 4. In cases not provided for in this Treaty, Argentine vessels will be subject to the rules of international law. During the passage, said vessels will refrain from carrying out any activity that is not directly related to the passage, such as the following: exercises or practices with weapons of any kind; launching, landing or receiving aircraft or military devices on board; embarkation or disembarkation of persons; fishing activities; research; hydrographic surveys; and activities that may disturb the security and communication systems of the Republic of Chile.

Article 5. Submarines and any other submersible vehicles must navigate on the surface. All ships will sail with lights on and flying their flag.

Article 6. The Republic of Chile may temporarily suspend the passage of ships in the event of an impediment to navigation due to force majeure and only for the time such impediment lasts. Said suspension will take effect once it has been communicated to the Argentine authority.

Article 7. The number of Argentine warships navigating simultaneously on the route described in Article 1 may not exceed three. Ships may not carry landing units on board. Navigation between Argentine ports in the Beagle Channel and Antarctica, and vice versa; or between Argentine ports in the Beagle Channel and the Argentine Exclusive Economic Zone adjacent to the maritime boundary between the Republic of Chile and the Argentine Republic, and vice versa.

Article 8. For maritime traffic between Argentine ports in the Beagle Channel and Antarctica, and vice versa; or between Argentine ports in the Beagle Channel and the Argentine Exclusive Economic Zone adjacent to the maritime boundary between the Republic of Chile and the Argentine Republic, and vice versa, Argentine vessels will enjoy navigation facilities for passage through Chilean internal waters exclusively by the following path: Picton and Richmond Passes following then, from the point fixed by the coordinates 55° 21', 0 South latitude and 66° 41', 0 West longitude, the general direction of the arc between 90° and 180° true geographic , to go out into the Chilean Territorial Sea; or crossing the Chilean Territorial Sea in the general direction of the arc between 270° and 000° true geographic, and continuing through the Richmond and Picton Passages. The pass will be carried out without a Chilean pilot or notice. The description of the aforementioned route is indicated in Letter Nº III attached.

Article 9. The provisions contained in articles 3, 4 and 5 of this Annex will be applied to the passage through the route indicated in the previous article. Navigation to and from the North through the Strait of Le Mair.

Article 10. For maritime traffic to and from the North through the Strait of Le Maire, Chilean ships will enjoy navigation facilities to pass through said Strait, without an Argentine pilot or notice. The provisions contained in articles 3, 4 and 5 of this Annex shall apply mutatis mutandis to the passage through this route.

Navigation, pilotage and pilotage regime in the Beagle Channel

Article 11. In the Beagle Channel, on both sides of the existing limit between the meridian 68° 36' 38.5" West longitude and the meridian 66° 25.0' West longitude indicated in Chart No. IV attached, the regime of navigation, pilotage and pilotage that is defined in the following articles.

Article 12. The Parties agree to freedom of navigation for Chilean and Argentine vessels in the section indicated in the previous article. In the indicated section, third-flag merchant ships will enjoy the right of passage subject to the rules established in this Annex.

Article 13. Third-flag warships heading to a port of one of the Parties located within the section indicated in Article 11 of this Annex, must have the prior authorisation of said Party. This will inform the other of the arrival or departure of a foreign warship.

Article 14. The Parties reciprocally agree to develop, in the section indicated in Article 11 of this Annex, in the areas that are under their respective jurisdictions, aids to navigation and to coordinate among themselves such aids in order to facilitate navigation and guarantee your safety. The usual navigation routes will be kept permanently clear of any obstacle or activity that may affect navigation. The Parties will agree on traffic management systems for the safety of navigation in geographic areas with difficult passage.

Article 15. Chilean and Argentine vessels are not required to take pilot in the section indicated in article 11 of this Annex. Vessels of third flags that sail from or to a port located in said section, must comply with the Pilotage and Pilotage Regulations of the country of the port of departure or destination. When said vessels navigate between ports of one Party and the other, they shall comply with the Pilotage Regulations of the Party of the port of departure and the Pilotage Regulations of the Party of the port of arrival.

Article 16. The Parties will apply their own regulations regarding Pilotage in the ports located in their respective jurisdictions. Vessels using pilots will host the flag of the country whose regulation they are applying. Any ship that uses pilotage and pilotage services must pay the corresponding fees for that service and any other tax that exists in this regard in the regulations of the Party that performs the pilotage and pilotage. The Parties will provide the pilots and pilots with the maximum facilities in the fulfilment of their mission. Said pilots or pilots may disembark freely in the ports of either Party. The Parties shall endeavour to establish consistent and uniform standards for pilotage.

Jaime del Valle Alliende   Dante Mario Caputo.

APPENDIX II

TABLE 3: Argentine Armed Forces Ranks (Officers)[12]		
Argentine Army	**Argentine Navy**	**Argentine Air Force**
Teniente General (Lieutenant General)	*Almirante* (Admiral)	*Brigadier General* (Brigadier General)
General de División (Major General)	*Vicealmirante* (Vice Admiral)	*Brigadier Mayor* (Brigadier Major)
General de Brigada (Brigadier General)	*Contraalmirante* (Rear Admiral)	*Brigadier* (Brigadier)
Coronel Mayor (Colonel Major)	*Comodoro de Marina* (Commodore of the Navy)	*Comodoro Mayor* (Commodore Major)
Coronel (Colonel)	*Capitán de Navío* (Captain)	*Comodoro* (Commodore)
Teniente Coronel (Lieutenant Colonel)	*Capitán de Fragata* (Commander)	*Vicecomodoro* (Vice Commodore)
Mayor (Major)	*Capitán de Corbeta* (Lieutenant Commander)	*Mayor* (Major)
Capitán (Captain)	*Teniente de Navío* (Ship Lieutenant)	*Capitán* (Captain)
Teniente Primero (First Lieutenant)	*Teniente de Fragata* (Frigate Lieutenant)	*Primer Teniente* (First Lieutenant)
Teniente (Lieutenant)	*Teniente de Corbeta* (Corvette Lieutenant)	*Teniente* (Lieutenant)
Subteniente (Sub-Lieutenant)	*Guardiamarina* (Midshipman)	*Alférez* (Ensign)

TABLE 4: Argentine Armed Forces Ranks (NCOs)[13]		
Argentine Army	**Argentine Navy**	**Argentine Air Force**
Sub Oficial Mayor (Chief Warrant Officer)	*Sub Oficial Mayor* (Master Chief Petty Officer)	*Sub Oficial Mayor* (Chief Warrant Officer)
Sub Oficial Principal (Deputy Chief Officer)	*Sub Oficial Principal* (Deputy Chief Officer)	*Sub Oficial Principal* (Deputy Chief Officer)
Sargento Ayudante (Assistant Sergeant)	*Sub Oficial Primero* (Chief Warrant Officer)	*Sub Oficial Ayudante* (Assistant Chief Officer)
Sargento Primero (First Sergeant)	*Sub Oficial Segundo* (Second Chief Warrant Officer)	*Sub Oficial Auxiliar* (Auxiliary Chief Officer)
Sargento (Sergeant)	*Cabo Principal* (Chief Corporal)	*Cabo Principal* (Chief Corporal)
Cabo Primero (First Corporal)	*Cabo Primero* (First Corporal)	*Cabo Primero* (First Corporal)
Cabo (Corporal)	*Cabo Segundo* (Second Corporal)	*Cabo Segundo* (Second Corporal)

TABLE 5: Argentine Armed Forces Ranks (Troops)[14]

Argentine Army	Argentine Navy	Argentine Air Force
Cadete (Cadet)	*Cadete* (Cadet)	*Cadete* (Cadet)
Aspirante (Aspirant)	*Aspirante* (Aspirant)	*Aspirante* (Aspirant)
Dragoneante (Dragoneant)	*Dragoneante* (Dragoneant)	*Dragoneante* (Dragoneant)
Soldado (Soldier)	*Conscripto* (Conscript)	*Soldado* (Soldier)

TABLE 6: Argentine Coast Guard Ranks[15]

Officers	NCOs
Prefecto General (General Prefect)	*Ayudante Mayor* (Senior Assistant)
Prefecto Mayor (Senior Prefect)	*Ayudante Principal* (Chief Assistant)
Prefecto Principal (Chief Prefect)	*Ayudante de Primera* (First Assistant)
Prefecto (Prefect)	*Ayudante de Segunda* (Second Assistant)
Sub Prefecto (Deputy Prefect)	*Ayudante de Tercera* (Third Assistant)
Oficial Principal (Chief Officer)	Cabo Primero (First Corporal)
Oficial Auxiliar (Auxiliary Officer)	Cabo Segundo (Second Corporal)
Oficial Ayudante (Assistant Officer)	Marinero (Sailor)

TABLE 7: Argentine National Gerdarmería Ranks[16]

Officers	NCOs
Comandante General (General Commander)	*Sub Oficial Mayor* (Chief Warrant Officer)
Comandante Mayor (Senior Commander)	*Sub Oficial Principal* (Deputy Chief Officer)
Comandante Principal (Main Commander)	*Sargento Ayudante* (Assistance Sergeant)
Segundo Comandante (Second Commander)	*Sargento Primero* (First Sergeant)
Primer Alférez (First Ensign)	*Sargento* (Sergeant)
Alférez (Ensign)	*Cabo Primero* (First Corporal)
Subalférez (Deputy Ensign)	*Cabo* (Corporal)
Cadete (Cadet)	*Aspirante a Sub Oficial* (NCO Aspirant)
-	*Gendarme* (Gendarme)
-	*Gendarme de Segunda* (second class Gendarme)

TABLE 8: Chilean Armed Forces Ranks (Officers)[17]

Chilean Army	Chilean Navy	Chilean Air Force
Comandante en Jefe/ Capitán General (Commander-in-Chief/Captain General)	The rank of Captain General, a 5-star General, was last used by President Pinochet, and did not have any equivalent in the Navy, Air Force and Carabineros.	
General de Ejército (Army General)	*Comandante en Jefe/Almirante* (Commander-in-Chief/Admiral)	*Comandante en Jefe/General del Aire* (Commander-in-Chief/Air General)
General de División (Major General)	*Vicealmirante* (Vice Admiral)	*General de Aviación* (Aviation General)
General de Brigada (Brigadier General)	*Contraalmirante* (Rear Admiral)	*General de Brigada Aérea* (Air Brigadier General)
Brigadier (Brigadier)	*Comodoro* (Commodore)	*Comodoro* (Commodore)
Coronel (Colonel)	*Capitán de Navío* (Captain)	*Coronel de Aviación* (Aviation Colonel)
Teniente Coronel (Lieutenant Colonel)	*Capitán de Fragata* (Commander)	*Comandante de Grupo* (Group Commander)
Mayor (Major)	*Capitán de Corbeta* (Lieutenant Commander)	*Comandante de Escuadrilla* (Squadron Commander)
Capitán (Captain)	*Teniente Primero* (First Lieutenant)	*Capitán de Bandada* (Group Captain)
Teniente Primero (First Lieutenant)	*Teniente Segundo* (Second Lieutenant)	*Teniente* (Lieutenant)
Teniente (Lieutenant)	*Sub Teniente* (Sub Lieutenant)	*Sub Teniente* (Sub Lieutenant)
Subteniente (Sub-Lieutenant)	*Guardiamarina* (Midshipman)	*Alférez* (Ensign)
Alférez (Ensign)	-	-

TABLE 9: Chilean Armed Forces ranks (NCOs)[18]

Chilean Army	Chilean Navy	Chilean Air Force
Sub Oficial Mayor (Chief Warrant Officer)	*Sub Oficial Mayor* (Master Chief Petty Officer)	*Sub Oficial Mayor* (Chief Warrant Officer)
Sub Oficial (Chief Officer)	*Sub Oficial* (Chief Officer)	*Sub Oficial* (Chief Officer)
Sargento Primero (First Sergeant)	*Sargento Primero* (First Sergeant)	*Sargento Primero* (First Sergeant)
Sargento Segundo (Second Sergeant)	*Sargento Segundo* (Second Sergeant)	*Sargento Segundo* (Second Sergeant)
Cabo Primero (First Corporal)	*Cabo Primero* (First Corporal)	*Cabo Primero* (First Corporal)
Cabo Segundo (Second Corporal)	*Cabo Segundo* (Second Corporal)	*Cabo Segundo* (Second Corporal)
Soldado Primero (First Soldier)	*Marinero Primero* (First Sailor)	*Cabo* (Corporal)

TABLE 10: Chilean Carabineros ranks[19]

Officers	NCOs
General Director (General Director)	*Sub Oficial Mayor* (Chief Warrant Officer)
General Sub Director y General Inspector (General Deputy Director & General Inspector)	*Sub Oficial* (Chief Officer)
General (General)	*Sargento Primero* (First Sergeant)
Coronel (Colonel)	*Sargento Segundo* (Second Sergeant)
Teniente Coronel (Lieutenant Colonel)	*Cabo Primero* (First Corporal)
Mayor (Major)	*Cabo Segundo* (Second Corporal)
Capitán (Captain)	*Carabinero* (Carabineer)
Teniente (Lieutenant)	-
Sub Teniente (Sub Lieutenant)	-

BIBLIOGRAPHY

Books

Academia de Historia Militar, *Ejército de Chile. Un recorrido por su historia* (Santiago: Ebooks Patagonia, 2020) (Digital ISBN: 978-956-8989-22-4)

Alvayay Castro, Enrique; Karel Blaha Rodríguez; Jorge Gutiérrez Garay; Reinaldo Reinike Espinoza & Javier Tortello Schuwirth, Vencer o Morir, *La fuerza de un juramento. Crisis de 1978* (Las Condes, Santiago: Amalfi Ediciones, 2021) (Digital ISBN: 978-956-6172-11-6)

Amores Oliver, Eduardo Juan, *Guía de Aeronaves Militares 1912–2006. Fuerza Aérea Argentina* (Buenos Aires: Dirección de Estudios Históricos. Fuerza Aérea Argentina, 2007) (ISBN: 978-987-24086-0-2)

Aranda Durañona, Comodoro (Ret.) Oscar Luis, *El Vuelo del Cóndor. Fuerza Aérea Argentina. 1912–2012. Cien años protegiendo nuestro cielo* (Buenos Aires: Dirección de Estudios Históricos de la Fuerza Aérea Argentina, 2012) (ISBN: 978-987-22106-6-3)

Arróspide Rivera, Julio & Raúl Zamora Martínez, *Del Vampire al Viper en la Fuerza Aérea de Chile, ¡Recargado! Segunda Edición* (Santiago de Chile: Aviation Art & History. Impresiones Valus, 2021) (ISBN: 978-956-09255-4-1)

Baldini, Atilio & Sergio Bontti, *El SA.315B Lama en la Fuerza Aérea Argentina. 1ª Edición* (Mendoza: Inca Editorial Cooperativa de Trabajo Ltda, 2003) (ISBN: 987-43-7017-3)

Baldini, Atilio & Jorge F. Núñez Padín, *North American F-86F-30-NA Sabre. Serie Fuerza Aérea #16* (Bahía Blanca: Ediciones Jorge Félix Núñez Padín, 2009) (ISBN: 978-987-20557-5-2)

Balza, General Martín Antonio & Mariano Grondona, *Dejo Constancia: Memorias de un General Argentino* (Buenos Aires: Editorial Planeta, 2001) (ISBN 950-49-0813-6)

Benadava, Santiago, *Recuerdos de la Mediación Pontificia entre Chile y Argentina (1978–1985)* (Santiago de Chile: Editorial Universitaria, 1999) (ISBN 956-11-1516-6)

Bulnes Serrano, Francisco & Patricia Arancibia Clavel, *La Escuadra En Acción* (Santiago de Chile: Editorial Grijalbo, 2004) (ISBN 956-258-211-6)

Burzaco, Ricardo, *Acorazados y Cruceros de la Armada Argentina, 1881–1982* (Buenos Aires: Eugenio B. Ediciones, 1997) (ISBN: 987-967-640-8)

Burzaco, Ricardo, *Submarinos de la Armada Argentina, 1933–2000* (Buenos Aires: Eugenio B. Ediciones, 1999) (ISBN: 978-987-9676-41-7)

Cáceres Godoy, Claudio & Jorge Félix Núñez Padín, *Hawker Hunter FGA.71/FR.71/T.72* (Buenos Aires: Ediciones Jorge Félix Núñez Padín, 1994)

Carmona, Guillermo Lagos, *Historia de las fronteras de Chile. Los tratados de límites con Argentina* (Santiago de Chile: Editorial Andrés Bello, 1980)

Correa Cuenca, Juan Manuel; Juan José Ahets Etcheverry; Luis Domingo Villar; Jorge Alberto Mones Ruiz & Oscar Luis Aranda Durañona, *Historia de la Fuerza Aérea Argentina. La Aviación de Caza (1912-1982)*, volume IV (Buenos Aires: Dirección de Estudios Históricos de la Fuerza Aérea Argentina, 2005)

Ejército de Chile, *Familia Acorazada del Ejército de Chile. Historia de los Vehículos Blindados del Ejército, 1936–2009* (Santiago de Chile: Talleres del Instituto Geográfico Militar, 2010)

Eló, Marcelo, Daniel Lillo, Alfredo Martínez, Diego Piedra & Francisco Sánchez, *1978 Operación Lanceros. Voces de los Centinelas de Última Esperanza*, 3ª Edición (Santiago de Chile: Authors' edition, 2020) (ISBN: 978-956-9839-08-5)

Francois, David, *Chile 1973. The Other 9/11. The Downfall of Salvador Allende* (Warwick: Helion & Company Ltd, 2018), eISBN: 978-1-913118-31-0

Granedis, Carlos & Marcos Olguín, *Alas de Pioneros: Historia del Grupo de Aviación No. 2 de la Fuerza Aérea de Chile*, Primera Edición (Santiago: Aviation Art & History, 2021) (ISBN: 978-956-0925-51-0)

Hagedorn, Dan & Mario Overall, *Douglas DC-3/C-47 in Latin America Military Service* (Manchester: Crécy Publishing Ltd, 2021) (ISBN: 978-1-91080-947-1)

Lacoste, Pablo, *La imagen del otro en las relaciones de la Argentina y Chile (1534–2000)* (Santiago de Chile: Fondo de Cultura Económica, Universidad de Santiago de Chile, 2003) (ISBN: 950-557-556-4)

López Tobar, *Mario: El 11 en la Mira de un Hawker Hunter* (Santiago: Editorial Sudamericana, 1999)

González Madariaga, Exequiel, *Nuestras relaciones con Argentina: Una historia deprimente. Del Tratado de Paz, Amistad, Comercio y Navegación, al Tratado de Límites de 1881* (Santiago de Chile: Editorial Andrés Bello, 1970)

Mellafe Maturana, Rafael, *Al borde de la Guerra, Chile-Argentina, 1978* (Santiago de Chile: Editorial Legatum, 2017) (ISBN: 978-956-9242-23-6)

Núñez Padín, Jorge F., *McDonnell Douglas A-4Q Skyhawk*, Serie Aeronaval No.11, 3ª Edición (Bahía Blanca: Ediciones Jorge Félix Núñez Padín, 2000)

Núñez Padín, Jorge F., *Dassault Mirage IIICJ/BJ & IIIEA/DA*. Serie Fuerza Aérea #23 (Bahía Blanca: Ediciones Jorge Félix Núñez Padín, 2013) (ISBN: 978-987-1682-21-8)

Núñez Padín, Jorge F., *IAI Dagger, 1978–1982, Parte 1*. Serie Fuerza Aérea Argentina #9 (Bahía Blanca: Ediciones Jorge Félix Núñez Padín, 2005)

Núñez Padín, Jorge F. & Sergio Pedroche, *Sikorsky S-61D.4 & UH-3H Sea King*, Serie Aeronaval #32 (Bahía Blanca: Ediciones Jorge Félix Núñez Padín, 2016) (ISBN: 978-987-1682-24-9)

Núñez Padín, Jorge F., *North American T-28 Fennec*, Serie Aeronaval #28 (Bahía Blanca: Ediciones Jorge Félix Núñez Padín, 2010)

Parvex, Guillermo, *La tormentosa historia limítrofe entre Chile y Argentina* (Santiago de Chile: Penguin Random House Grupo Editorial S.A., 2022) (ISBN: 978-956-6056-89-8)

Passarelli, Bruno, *El Delirio Armado: Argentina-Chile la Guerra que Evitó el Papa* (Buenos Aires: Editorial Sudamericana, 1998) (ISBN 950-07-1469-8)

Pavlovcic, Gabriel & Esteban Raczynski, *Helicópteros en la Fuerza Aérea Argentina. Historia y Legado, 1ª Edición Especial* (Buenos Aires: Artes Gráficas del Sur S.R.L., 2022) (ISBN: 978-987-88-3709-3)

Rivas, Santiago, *Northrop C/F-5A/B/E/F en Latinoamérica*, Serie Latin Wings #1 (Bahía Blanca: Ediciones Jorge Félix Núñez Padín, 2012) (ISBN: 978-987-1682-15-7)

Rojas, Arturo Nahuel, *Veteranos de 1978. Relatos de los protagonistas*, 1st Edition (Santiago de Chile: Legatum Editores, 2020)

Rousseaux, Prefecto General (RE) Andrés René, *La Prefectura Naval Argentina en el Teatro de Operaciones Austral, 1978–1979* (Buenos Aires: Editorial Guardacostas, 1998) (ISBN: 987-95927-6-X)

Rousseaux, Prefecto General (RE) Andrés René, *Historia de las embarcaciones de la Prefectura Naval Argentina*, Tomo III 1950–1982 (Buenos Aires: Prefectura Naval Argentina, 2012)

Sánchez Urra, Francisco, *Los Soldados del Mar en Acción: La infantería de Marina y la defensa de la soberanía Austral, 1958–1978*, 10ª Edición. Colección Historia Militar y Pensamiento Estratégico (Santiago de Chile: Círculo Acton Chile Ediciones, 2020) (ISBN: 978-956-9839-08-5)

Sequeira, Sebastián; Carlos Cal & Cecilia Catalayub, *Aviación Naval Argentina* (Mendoza: SS & CC Ediciones, 1984) (ISBN: 978-950-9064-02-7)

Sigal Fogliani, Ricardo Jorge, *Blindados Argentinos, de Uruguay y Paraguay* (Buenos Aires: Editorial Ayer y Hoy Ediciones, 1997)

Sigal Fogliani, Ricardo Jorge, *El Sherman en el Ejército Argentino* (Buenos Aires: 1884 Editorial Círculo Militar, 2014) (ISBN: 978-987-4112-13-2)

Siminic Ossio, Iván, Rojo 1. *La Fuerza Aérea de Chile en la crisis del Beagle de 1978*, Primera Edición. (Santiago de Chile: Academia de Guerra Aérea, 2021) (ISBN: 978-956-09714-0-1)

Vio Valdivieso, Fabio, *La mediación de su S.S. el Papa Juan Pablo II* (Santiago de Chile: Editorial Aconcagua, 1984)

Articles

'Archivo de la Legión de Infantería de Marina: Desafíos del Cuerpo de Infantería de Marina ante la crisis del Beagle de 1978,' in *Revista Mar – Órgano de Difusión de la Liga Marítima de Chile*, Nr.205, 2019 (Valparaíso: 2019) (ISSN: 0047-5866)

Burzaco, Ricardo, 'La fuerza de submarinos de la Armada Argentina en la Crisis de 1978', in *Revista Defensa y Seguridad*, Nr.43 (Buenos Aires)

Fernández Rodríguez, Arturo, '1978: Vivencias de quienes estuvieron en las trincheras', in *Perspectivas de Historia Militar of the Academia de Historia Militar*, December 2018 (Santiago de Chile: 2018)

Morán, Teniente de Fragata Sebastián Emiliano, 'Los Pactos de Mayo. La Paz Entre Países Hermanos' Departamento de Estudios Históricos Navales, Armada Argentina

McIntyre Astorga, Vicealmirante Ronald, '1978: La Guerra que no fue. Un análisis 40 años después', in *Revista Mar – Órgano de Difusión de la Liga Marítima de Chile*, Nr.205, 2019 (Valparaíso: 2019) (ISSN: 0047-5866)

Ostornol Varela, Capitán de Navío Sergio, La Guerra antes de la Guerra', in *Revista Mar – Órgano de Difusión de la Liga Marítima de Chile*, Nr. 205, 2019 (Valparaíso, 2019) (ISSN: 0047-5866)

Pulgar Neira, Sergio Hermann & Miguel A. Hervé Claude, 'Historia, Perfiles, Fotos y Planos del Douglas DC-6A/B cuatrimotor de transporte del Grupo de Aviación Nro. 10 de la FACH, 1966-1981, Dossier Histórico Modelístico' (Santiago de Chile: Editorial Histórico Modelística. Santiago de Chile, 2005)

Timmermann, Freddy, 'Racionalidades de la guerra y la paz. Argentina-Chile 1977-1984' in *Cuadernos de Historia 29* (Santiago: Departamento de Ciencias Históricas. Universidad de Chile, Septiembre 2008)

Werner Cavada, Eduardo, 'Medios Aéreos embarcados en la Armada de Chile', in *Boletín Nr. 18, Museo Nacional*

Aeronáutico y del Espacio, Dirección General de Aeronáutica Civil, 2019 (Santiago de Chile, 2019) (ISSN: 0719-0239)

Zamora, Raúl y Javier Carrera, ''La Fuerza Aérea de Chile en la Crisis del Beagle' in *Revista Enfoque Estratégico, 22 de febrero de 2008* (Santiago, 2008)

Zegers Ariztía, Cristian, 'Conflicto con Argentina 1978: Proceso político y diplomatic,' in *Revista Mar – Órgano de Difusión de la Liga Marítima de Chile*. Nr. 205, 2019 (Valparaíso, 2019) (ISSN: 0047-5866)

Newspapers

Martinic, Ivan, 'La Fuerza de Submarinos de la Armada de Chile en el conflicto de 1978,' (Santiago de Chile: Article published in *Diario El Mercurio*)

Web Pages

Argentine Army Aviation in https://loudandclearisnotenought. blogspot.com/p/ejercito-argentino-cuando-el-4.html

Argentine Air Force, Naval Aviation, Army Aviation, Prefectura Naval Aviation and Gendarmeria Aviation data in https:// www.amilarg.com.ar/index.html

Fundación Histarmar, Historia y Arqueología Marítima: 'Buques de la Armada Argentina, 1900–2017' in www. histarmar.com.ar

Fundación Histarmar, Historia y Arqueología Marítima: "Aviación Naval Argentina" in www.histarmar.com.ar

https://crisisbeagle.blogspot.com/2015/03/alberto-n-manfredi-h_24.html

Carabineros de Chile Aviation in https://www.capecar. cl/historia/

Chilean Naval Aviation history in
https://www.defensa.com/en-abierto/perspectiva-historica-aviacion-naval-chile

https://aviationrainbows.com/2018/05/27/la-aviacion-naval-de-la-armada-de-chile/

Chilean Navy ships in
https://www.armada.cl/tradicion-e-historia/unidades-historicas/unidades-historicas

Argentine & Chilean armament in https:// aquellasarmasdeguerra.wordpress.com/

'Demining process in Chile' in https://www.defensa.com/chile/avanza-el-desminado-en-chile/

Conference

Bravo Valdivieso, Germán, Buques de la Armada construidos en Chile. Santiago de Chile: Lecture given on 28 March 2006

NOTES

Chapter 1

1 Vladimiro Cettolo, *Historical Record of the Douglas A-4C Skyhawk in the Argentine Air Force, 1975–1999*. Chapter VIII, under the title Bautismo Sobre las Sguas del Pacífico, pp.9–10.

2 Siminic Ossio, Iván, Rojo 1. *La Fuerza Aérea de Chile en la crisis del Beagle de 1978*. Primera Edición, (Santiago: Academia de Guerra Aérea, 2021).

Chapter 2

1 Enrique Bernstein Carabantes, *Recuerdos de un diplomático ante el Papa mediador 1979–1982*, Vol. IV, (Santiago de Chile: Editorial Andrés Bello, 1989.)

2 *Historia General de las Relaciones Exteriores de Argentina.*

3 *casus belli* (lit. cause for war) is the Latin referring to the reason for war; an act of war that provokes or is used to justify a war.

4 *El año que vivimos en peligro, Revista Capital No.237*, 17 de Septiembre al 2 de Octubre de 2008.

5 *El año que vivimos en peligro, Revista Capital No.237*, 17 de Septiembre al 2 de Octubre de 2008.

Chapter 3

1 A 'jab' is a boxing term meaning a straight blow to the opponent with the hand projected at the height of the chin.

2 An 'uppercut' is another boxing term meaning a blow thrown from the bottom up and in the direction of the opponent's chin, usually in close fighting.

Chapter 4

1 Ivan Martinic, 'La Fuerza de Submarinos de la Armada de Chile en el conflicto de 1978,' in *El Mercurio* newspaper, Santiago de Chile.

Chapter 5

1 https://www.elsnorkel.com/2008/11/la-fuerza-de-submarinos-de-la-armada.html

Chapter 6

–

Appendix II:

Table 3
12 https://www.fuerzas-armadas.mil.ar/GradosMilitares.aspx

Table 4
13 https://www.fuerzas-armadas.mil.ar/GradosMilitares.aspx

Table 5
14 https://www.fuerzas-armadas.mil.ar/GradosMilitares.aspx

Table 6
15 https://www.argentina.gob.ar/prefecturanaval/jerarquias

Table7
16 https://www.argentina.gob.ar/jerarquias-de-gendarmeria-nacional

Table 8
17 https://www.guiature.cl/equivalencia-cargos-grados-instituciones.html

Table 9
18 https://www.guiature.cl/equivalencia-cargos-grados-instituciones.html

Table 10
19 https://www.guiature.cl/equivalencia-cargos-grados-instituciones.html

ABOUT THE AUTHOR

Antonio Luis Sapienza Fracchia was born in Asunción, Paraguay on 14 May 1960. He graduated from the Catholic University of Asunción where he received a B.A. in Clinical Psychology. He also took specialised English courses at Tulane University of New Orleans, Louisiana, and teaching methodology at San Diego State University in California. He is now retired but for 40 years worked as an English Teacher and one of the Academic Co-ordinators at the Centro Cultural Paraguayo-Americano (CCPA), a binational institute in Asunción. Married with two children, he resides in the capital.

He is an Aviation Historian who has written more than 500 articles in specialised magazines and on web pages on Paraguayan Aviation history, he has given numerous lectures in schools, universities, institutes, military and civil institutions in Paraguay and abroad. Since 2010, he has been an aviation history professor in the Paraguayan Air Force (FAP). He has published 22 books since 1996, this one being his tenth with Helion. He received a total of six decorations for his academic merits, two from Argentina, one from Brazil and three from his home country of Paraguay.